Shopping in Jail

Ideas, Essays, and Stories for the Increasingly Real Twenty-First Century

Douglas Coupland

Sternberg Press

Consider this: we are defined by data more than we are by our red blood cells, raging hormones, and militantly groomed body hair (or not, depending). Our data selves are a string of random facts; searchable, downloadable, marketable—but not erasable. Unless, as Douglas Coupland suggests, we destroy the Cloud—that ethereal-sounding totality of server farms in darkened spaces that contain the digital doppelgänger of our world. Or maybe, it's our world that's the doppelgänger now, echoing what Philip K. Dick once wondered: "What if our world is their heaven?"

3　　When we want to know who or what a person is, we type their name in an elongated window on our screen, tap [ENTER], and see what surfaces. Hearsay, biographical facts, digital debris, costume disasters—all of which will never be allowed to die. A person is the sum totality of this chronologically flattened constellation. Herein is a spurious list describing the author of the ensuing book. Some of the following is out there in the Googlesphere. Most of it is just between you and me.

- He was born on a military base in Germany. This—and the fact that his child- and early adulthood happened under the Cold War's ambient, tangible threat—could be why apocalypse is never far away from his work.
- He worked on a TV series in which every episode ended with the end of the world.
- His novel *Girlfriend in a Coma* imagines the world ending by everyone falling asleep, person by person.
- He thinks he's underproductive but, in fact, he's incalculably prolific. It's as though he's worried the world will end by midnight, tonight. *Better get stuff done.*
- He's prolific in words and images and, lately, public sculpture. In Toronto, he's made a 3-D killer whale look like a low-res 2-D JPEG. Things are images. Images are often poor quality.
- He also treats words as images. It may have to do with his time apprenticing in design

magazines. It may have to do with how his brain is wired.

- He wrote about Marshall McLuhan's brain in his biography of the Canadian media theorist. (McLuhan was exceptionally wired: he had a third artery in his head that ran through his brain's left lobe. It made blood flow twice as fast as the rest of us.)
- He is the heir apparent of McLuhan—for the Internet and, now, post-Internet world.
- He loves macaroni and cheese. "It's brain fuel."

Doug has been sending me bulletins from his garden in West Vancouver since we first met. Typically, it includes a description of the daily temperature, the kind of daylight, and what the squirrels and jaybirds are up to. These bulletins always sound like that day is the only day that's ever happened. Time is a commodity whose value can rise and fall unexpectedly.

- He feels the present moment ultra-vividly.
- He once said, "The past sucks."
- He wishes he'd written Eric Hobsbawm's *The Age of Extremes: The Short Twentieth Century, 1914–1991*. It's a book about the past.
- He lived and worked in Japan in the 1980s when it still felt like the future of the world. He didn't visit New York till the 1990s. He went to Dubai for the first time in 2012. He tells me that it's clear the future today is a

lot more east than it was at the end of the twentieth century.

The bullet points I'm using here as a rhetorical device are commonly found in corporate documents. Doug's novels *Microserfs*, *J-Pod*, and *The Gum Thief* all pay attention to the humdrum details of where modern humans work: the office, the cubicle, the warehouse. Because most of your life is spent not in the throes of sublime aesthetic ecstasy. It's being bored. Which is why beautiful things—like art you love, or love itself—become so important. They can make life feel, temporarily, like it should feel. Alive.

- He went to art school in the early 1980s.
- He cites Jenny Holzer's *Truisms* as an impetus to write. He aphorizes effortlessly. In fact, he was effectively tweeting decades before Twitter even began.
- He stopped making art in the 1990s after *Generation X* became a hit. "You can't be a serious author if you're an artist too," was the kind of binary advice back then.
- He resumed art making in the 2000s. Writing and art happen in parallel now. They use different parts of the brain. Sometimes you need to escape—to the wordless part (a play of colors, shapes, symbols, icons)—to get back to the words. And sometimes a tribute to Andy Warhol's wigs is enough.

- He confided that the art world (its artists, curators, critics) allow for pluralistic conversations in a way that isn't as apparent in the literary world. He has a mind that digresses—*hyperlinks*—between disciplines, generations, agendas. Art does this in a way that makes him feel at home.
- He makes art from languages he doesn't speak. Languages are visual things.
- He introduced the word "smupid" in 2013. It's a fusion of smart and stupid. He constantly invents new words, neologisms, and acronyms. Reality, I reckon, needs to be described before we fully recognize it as reality.
- He needs to invent a word that describes the sensation of going from very happy to very sad very quickly. And back again.

There is every arbitrary chance that this random sample of things about Douglas Coupland is also about you.

Shopping in Jail

Ideas, Essays, and Stories
for the Increasingly
Real Twenty-First Century

Douglas Coupland

ISBN 978-3-943365-86-3
130 × 195 mm
92 pages, 10 euros

9 783943 365863

Sternberg Press

On American reality TV shows they'll sometimes interview a teenager about something that's just happened to them on the show; perhaps this teenager has just finished eating a smoothie made of tropical insects, or perhaps they've just karaoked with Demi Moore. More often than not, these young people will say, "It was so ... *surreal*." This comes as a shock to me because these are people who can't locate France on a world map or multiply 8 × 7, and yet here they are using the word "surreal."

Awesome—it was so surreal.

So what exactly *is* it these young people actually mean when they stare at a game-show host and say, "Wow, that was so surreal—I can't believe I just smashed cantaloupe melons with Grace Jones"? Traditionally, surrealism is about images and symbols inside our brains free-associating with themselves without the burden or agenda of day-to-day consciousness. Not quite a dream state; rather, a recognition that there are deeper levels of identity available that can be accessed creatively with the goal of crystallizing new and revealing mental states in the form of an artwork or artistic experience.

The collective assumption here is that deeper and truer versions of ourselves do exist—wiser, deeper versions. If only we could listen attentively enough, we might become better humans, far more engaged with being alive on this planet, less sexually screwed up, more fully creative: hence Sigmund Freud and everything since. But there are potential errors in this system of thinking.

In Vienna in the mid-1990s I was giving a lecture at the Vienna Literary Festival, and the theme that year was money. When I came on stage, I said, "It's a pleasure to be visiting Vienna, the place where the subconscious was invented." I waited a second for that to sink in. There was a bit of a murmur, at which point I said, "*Whoops.* What I meant to say was that it's a pleasure to be in Vienna, the place where the subconscious was *discovered.*" That made everyone quiet and happy; the existence of the subconscious was nonnegotiable. Later in that same talk I mentioned how the subconscious is actually a lot like Antarctica: it's huge, we know very little about it, it's incredibly hard to reach, and it can be visited only if you have access to lots of money. Rather than getting a chuckle, people rubbed their chins and made body language to the effect of, "This Canadian writer chap has made a very good point. Bravo."

After Vienna I began thinking about the subconscious on a scientific level: id, ego, and superego.

But why just the three levels? Maybe there are six levels of the self. Or a few hundred. Or an infinite number. To date, I've read no satisfying scientific reason to assume a mere three levels of self. It may well be true; I just don't believe it. It's things like SSRI antidepressants and other pills developed in the last two decades that make me wonder if the psyche is infinitely layered and ever evolving. Concepts change. An example? We once believed that as adults we had all the brain cells we're ever going to have inside our skulls, and that from puberty on, we can only lose them. But no, we all grow about 10,000 new cells a day, with the caveat that unless we use them, these new cells are reabsorbed back into the body (which is kind of surreal). Serves us right for not using them.

But here I've only discussed levels of self and identity looking inward. What makes 2012 so much more interesting than 1912 is that we now have this thing called the Internet in our lives, and this Internet thingy has, in the most McLuhanistic sense, become a true externalization of our interior selves: our memories, our emotions, so much of our entire sense of being and belonging. The Internet has taken something that was once inside us and put it outside of us, has made it searchable, mashable, stealable, and tinkerable. The Internet, as described by William Gibson, is a massive consensual hallucination, and at this point in history, not too many people would disagree.

But let's go back in time a few decades. Let's go back to 1981, my second year in art school, pre-Prozac, pre-personal computer, pre- many things. I remember being told by instructors that changing the channels on a TV set just to see what juxtapositions it throws back at you was postmodern because one wasn't dealing with a true subconsciousness, it was a pseudo-consciousness, and therefore not interesting. I disagreed violently, and continue to. It presupposes an inability of human consciousness to expand outside of itself; Greece and Rome had civilizations, and Vancouver in 1981 had changing TV channels; older civilizations may be more glamorous and enduring, but ontologically, they're no different than TV channel changes. Television is ephemeral; the Colosseum is concrete but still corroding; it's only a matter of time frames. Collective manifestation of the inner world can, and does, take infinite forms.

Which gets us back to surrealism proper, and it gets us back to teenagers on American TV saying, "Wow, man, that was the most surreal experience." What these teenagers are alluding to, it seems to me, is that their psyches have been put through an external identity randomizer—they've been pulled through the churn. The game show or reality show or what have you has taken the teenager on a tour through externalized layers of reality that are utterly new since 1912, 1981, or even 2000. Their psyches have been whisked through the collective dream and the collective subconscious, yielding just the same sorts of tingly sensations one might have had looking at a Salvador Dalí or a René Magritte in the 1920s or 1930s.

It's also important to remember that Surrealism was a movement. In the early twentieth century, movements lasted decades. By the 1960s, they lasted two years. Nowadays we don't even have movements; we have *memes*. Memes last a day or two and then vanish. Were Surrealism to have been invented today, it would be a very cool website that throws images and clips together and makes your head feel tingly. "Have you gone to supersurrealism.com? It's like a Japanese TV game show except it's for real and it's exploding right in front of your face. It's totally supersurreal."

1

In the early 1990s I was in Los Angeles on a book tour and staying in hotel on the Sunset Strip, a hotel then called the St. James Club—a nineteen-story art-deco pile built in 1929, then recently refurbished with great pretentions to chic. I was elevatoring down to my room around dinnertime, and I saw that the state of California had implemented mandatory anti-smoking plaques on the walls in the hallway outside the doors saying words to the effect that smoking causes cancer in unborn children—or words equally overkill and medical. The plaques were bronze and really quite beautifully made, but, I mean, even back when people smoked, they still never smoked in *elevators*.

This is all to say that I found the anti-smoking plaques redolent of a certain sensibility gone horribly wrong: the government meets the insurance oligarchy meets a junior interior designer in a corporate in-house design studio who has a memo dropped onto their desk saying, "We have to hang this sign, like it or not, so make it look good: this is California and people expect swankiness at the St. James Club."

Voilà … the little bronze sign was born.

I actually found this sign so utterly weird that I wanted to make a rubbing of it to post on my "tour diary"—basically, a proto-blog back in the days where there was an Internet, except there wasn't really anywhere to go on it yet. And this was also the early 1990s, so making a pencil rubbing and posting it on a blog wasn't a simple proposition. These days, a casual iPhone snap would suffice for a blog but back then, a posting like this was making a commitment to an image: I'd have to make the rubbing, FedEx it back to my Vancouver office, have them scan it, and from there it could be posted—slow, laborious, and expensive. But before I could begin, first I'd have to find a *pencil*, which was the hardest task of all; even in the early 1990s, outside of golf courses, pencils had come close to extinction. There was no pencil in my travel bag or the hotel room, so I went to the front desk to ask. There was a kid working there—twenty?—he seemed awfully young to be working the front desk in a good hotel, but it was California, and he could be forty and had a lot of good work done on him, so who knew. I asked him for a pencil and he took the task to heart. "Yes sir!" He bustled about the desk and in the room behind the desk, and was brimming with cheer when he appeared with the remains of half a pencil covered with corn-like bite marks all along its flanks. It was offered to me like a frail baby chick, but while I was thanking him, I noticed the pencil was dull, and asked if he had a sharpener.

More bustling.

After perhaps three minutes he said, "No sharpener, sir, but if you hang on a second, I can get it sharpened for you." At this point I was so heavily invested in the pencil experience, there was no way I was going to leave, so I stood at the counter while Junior went off to sharpen his pencil. (Doesn't *that* sound like sexual innuendo?) But after maybe five minutes, time was ticking on and I really did have to leave, so I headed out the front door only to find, out on the Sunset Strip, Junior rubbing the pencil on the pavement, sharpening its point as though it were a spear being sharpened on a boulder, while rush-hour cars sped past. Junior was oblivious to the cars and to me and the world; he was a man with a mission—and a man with a five-dollar tip in his future—but until he received his tip, I stood watching him crouched on the Sunset curb, his arms rubbing back and forth, sharpening, sharpening, sharpening, and I was thinking to myself, "Yes, this truly is an Ed Ruscha moment."

Artists reframe our world in ways that allow us to aestheticize what previously was *just* the world. Andy Warhol said that once you saw the world as Pop, you could never look at it the same way again, and he was right. Ed Ruscha cast the same sort of spell with his own sensibility, one often short-handed as "LA," or "Southern California," but which is, in fact, much larger and not so LA-centric. One might begin describing Ruscha's realm as being that of a window in time, from the end of World War II up to the first hippie, and from a certain place, the North American West, perhaps minus San Francisco and everything northward. It was a time and a place that perceived itself culturally as being ahistorical; culture came from the East Coast or from Europe or from anywhere else but there. Yes, there was Hollywood, but film production was tinged with an industrial ethos and felt not unlike the Kaiser steel facilities sixty miles inland in Fontana—a city one has no choice but to drive through when migrating to the coast from, say, Oklahoma, Ruscha's childhood home. And thus we see multiple cofactors jelling together: a time and a place riven with countless military, industrial, and cultural signifiers, all baking in both smog and a sense of disconnection with the realm of high culture production—this to me is Ruschaworld, and when he writes, this is what comes to mind.

2

In 1995 I was working with *Wired* magazine doing a special issue on the "Future." One of my topics was the Future of Garbage and I was into this topic because of the time shifts intrinsic to it. The moment you declare an object to be garbage, it immediately enters the past tense and it becomes instant archaeology. Because it's "only garbage" you don't overthink the trashing process, so you can often find very interesting portraits of a person by looking only at what they discard. It's very different from thinking about the future. The moment you start thinking about the world in front of you as being in the future, the world is revealed in a radiant new light, sort of like wearing 3-D or infrared glasses. So to look at trash with futurological lenses is kind of like a temporal double-whammy.

This trash project came up just before a week I had to spend in Los Angeles. I had thought the week in LA would be filled with creativity and industry, but it instead devolved that West Coast randomness where everyone was driving, and driving, and driving, and trying to figure out where to go for lunch or dinner or a drink. I was with a posse that week and was determined to be sociable and relax a little, but the driving and aimlessness was driving me nuts, so I arranged for a ride from a friend who'd pick me up by Book Soup at the corner of Sunset and Larabee. This was pre-cell phone, so arranging pickups and drop-offs was a complex, boring, and heavily orchestrated task. In the end, I ended up sitting on a bench with actor Stephen Dorff who was going to the same place as me. We had time to kill and I started discussing the project on the future and he actually grew enthusiastic, which I liked. Ever since art school, I've always been suspicious of anyone who is reluctant to go dumpster diving, as no other activity so succinctly reveals your fundamental level of curiosity. Basically: dumpsters are great big stinky ids just begging to be explored.

But before Stephen and I dumpster dove, we started with a simple, almost-full municipal trashcan. Science has many laws, and so does urban archaeology; one of its inviolable laws is that in any Sunset Strip trash can you will always find fried-chicken remains and a pair of used underwear—and our trash can was no different. Bored of the predictable, we then wanted to up our game; we looked down the street and saw alleys with genuine dumpsters and decided, "Why not?" So we went on a dig.

That part of LA is heavily peppered with film and TV production offices, and the block by Sunset and Larabee (the Viper Room is there) was no exception. Our first dumpster yielded a trove of unshredded scripts laced with notes from whomever was doing coverage on them. Most of the notes were generic, like: "weak," or "pass." There was one funny one I remember: "needs defibrillators."

Stephen and I were essentially wallowing in a form of industrial waste, except instead of leftover plastics or metal we were wallowing in a container load of crushed dreams and failed hopes and it felt kind of decadent being there: crush, crush, crush; rip, rip, rip. In another universe I would have set fire to the scripts but not in this one. Instead we walked back up the surprisingly steep hill to the Strip and inside the reptile stem of my brain reverberated the words: *Ed Ruscha*.

3

In the late 1980s I ended up in Palm Springs, California, back before its current incarnation as a gay mid-century fantasia. The '80s were ending, and so was communism. I remember removing the *LA Times* from the newspaper box outside of Sunshine Deli the day the Soviet Union ended. I remember reading it inside surrounded by seniors eating grapefruit and Sanka and feeling how disconnected this scenario was from the rest of the species (of how disconnected all those grapefruits were), and, outside the deli, how disconnected the trophy lawns were—and the Chrysler LeBarons with handicapped stickers and the piped-in EZ-listening music that's as omnipresent in Palm Springs as the smell of citrus blossoms and malathion.

Disconnection was the key word in my life at that period. I had an ancient VW fastback and I drove around the desert listening to Stone Roses and New Order cassettes feeling as though the time had come to an end and we were collectively entering one great big endless cultural flea market, a post-era era.

I wanted to do a visual piece that embodied this asteroidal sense of timelessness, and I decided on renting a VHS recorder from a place in Palm Desert for a specific shoot I had in mind—I wanted to film a pile of books being buried in the desert. I liked the poetry of it, and it's one of those impulses it's best not to fight because it usually leads to other ideas that might be much better.

My technical assistant and model for the shoot was a girl, Marie, who worked at a long-gone Brentano's Books on North Palm Canyon Drive. On a Sunday (like days of the week matter in Palm Springs) we drove out Indian Canyon Boulevard, maybe ten miles out toward the wind-turbine farms where Indian Canyon hits the 10.

In order for Marie to not think I was crazy and secretly asking her to dig her own grave, we stayed within sightline of the road, and she began to dig a hole, camera running. It was pretty straightforward: once the hole was dug, she was to then throw some books in the hole, and replenish the hole with dirt. What I hadn't counted on was how susceptible Marie was to the sun, and once she'd dug a hole big enough to entomb a Barbie doll at best, she promptly bent over and threw up into the hole.

Shoot over.

Marie returned to the VW. I quickly threw the books onto the tiny hole and shoveled dirt on top of them. We drove back into town, and twenty-two years later I still wonder about those books and all that puke and wonder what happened to it. Did it feed the roots of a creosote shrub or a cholla cactus or an ant colony? Did the sun blow away the dirt and fry it all into dust within a year or two? Or, most likely, did it all, in the end, mummify and become a time capsule? That's what happens when you create an object or make a gesture in the middle of nowhere. You have the freedom to do whatever you want, but your actions happen in a vacuum, outside of culture and outside of cultural time. I wonder if Ruscha ever felt like that, especially in Los Angeles in the 1950s. In his head, was he shooting his work in a capsule headed into outer space with no particular destination, never to return? Or was he shooting out ropes and tethers to bind LA and the ahistorical west to the supercontinent of cultural history? Maybe both; maybe neither. The days move on. Grapefruits are eaten. Sanka is drunk. Chicken bones are thrown away. The LACMA builds a new wing. Words are spoken. Words are recorded and then they are erased. Occasionally only the fragments survive, only the shards, maybe a few stray words here and there, and maybe that's all that's ever really required.

We now inhabit a decidedly post-Koonsian world where, as we know, if anybody can be an artist, then anything can be art. Everyone is creative. Everyone makes art. Art, art, art! We're entering an a sort of post-era era where the driving force of everyday life is the continuing pursuit of what writer William Gibson calls "curated novelty."

And even in this new realm, bad art is still art. We know this because we are wise and tolerant and can take bad art in stride. And non-art? Even non-art, we know, is art by default: a readymade!

And yet...

And yet there is something causing unease amid this artstravaganza. There is one sabot to be thrown into the machinery of the curated twenty-first century lifestyle, and this is *craft*.

Craft?

You can't be serious.

Craft is not art. Craft is skill-based. Craft is sentimental. Craft has no theoretical rigor. Craft means that (one must grudgingly admit) a creative person has chosen to limit his or her expression to one medium—*one medium*—in a post-medium world where it is only the idea that is permitted to generate form.

But, like African animals forced to inhabit the same veldt, craft and art manage to coexist without bloodshed, oftentimes overlapping only in the shared oasis of the gift shop.

And the years tick on.

In the 1970s the realm of art began to strobe and flicker with video installations, lightscapes, and soundscapes. *Isms* of all sorts flourished and multiplied. To walk into a contemporary art museum anywhere on earth, one has now come to expect by rote the walled-off room containing flickering and squawking images projected by a highly lumened digital projector, or empty floor space with perhaps some chalk outlines or a piece of string and, well, the problem here is the word "rote." Or, perhaps the problem here is the phrase "come to expect." One now often feels let down by the contemporary art museum unless it delivers to us a set of objects and experiences that feels like modern art—which is the exact opposite of what modern art is intended to be. This would seem to indicate that the contemporary museum is increasingly missing the mark in fulfilling its agenda of generating the new. Paul Valéry wrote, "Any view of things that is not strange is false," and by this standard, one might say that many modern art institutions are on their way to becoming factories of falseness. This type of prattling is just the sort of discussion best held over the remains of what's in the wine bottle after a Saturday night dinner. But one point that does seem to be a little bit undeniable now is that contemporary art seems to be sputtering a bit—much of it is starting to look old-fashioned—which is, in its own way, exciting, because it means modern art is shortly due for a reimagining, which is why it exists, so hurray for sputtering.

And enter the next generation of craft: skill married with what seems to be critical rigor, decided political stances, and a willingness to let the medium be an overt part of the message, a willingness that, in the presence of an increasingly arid conceptual realm, now feels almost radical.

Of course, novelty for the sake of novelty is stupid and decadent, but novelty that reflects the powerful but less prominent forces of any culture is interesting and worthy of exploration. Cultures shift; technology morphs. Aesthetic experiences and objects are now dividing into the binary categories of downloadable and non-downloadable. The new museums being built are ones that focus on the digital, causing a necessary reevaluation of what happens with physical things. One can look at some of the contemporary art being made and reclassify it by saying that rather than it being art, it is folk art that uses modernist vernaculars as its medium. Similarly, one can reclassify some contemporary "craft" as art objects that deploy craftsmanship as their medium. It's wordplay, but it's increasingly more relevant wordplay. Grade school students know the difference between Garamond and Times New Roman. Anyone with a basement has probably made a CD of themselves making and/or mixing something musical. Advertising clients walk into agencies on Monday morning and say, "This is what my kid did on the weekend, and here's what you charged me a quarter-million dollars for. What's the difference?"

I see a happy emergence in this exhibition, a sense of something true being kept alive during hard times, a meeting of ideas, materials, and the soul—and a wave of reclassification that shows only signs of growing. The crafts shown here have lost their sentimentality and gained in rigor. In an ever-flattening world of downloaded nonphysical experiences, the crafted object is in the ascendant, and ultimately might prove to be the trunk of the tree that gives rise to the next dominant wave of modern art. This is a win-win scenario with the added bonus that it does indeed seem to be the future, and one we can only increasingly anticipate.

One thing that struck me about the 9/11 footage shown during last year's anniversary was that in 2001, the people on New York City's sidewalks had no smartphones with which to record the events of the day. History may well look back on 9/11 as the world's last underdocumented mega-event. But aside from the absence of phone cameras, the people and streets of September 2001 looked pretty much identical to those of September 2011: the clothes, the hair, the cars. I mention this because it has been only in the past decade that we appear to have entered an aura-free universe in which all eras coexist at once—a state of possibly permanent atemporality given to us courtesy of the Internet. No particular era now dominates. We live in a post-era era without forms of its own powerful enough to brand the times. The zeitgeist of 2012 is that we have a lot of *Zeit* but not much *Geist*. I can't believe I just wrote that last sentence, but it's true; there is something psychically sparse about the present era, and artists of all stripes are responding with fresh strategies.

This new reality seems to have manifested in the literary world in what must undeniably be called a new literary genre. For lack of a better word, let's call it Translit. Translit novels cross history without being historical; they span geography without changing psychic place. Translit collapses time and space as it seeks to generate narrative traction in the reader's mind. It inserts the contemporary reader into other locations and times, while leaving no doubt that its viewpoint is relentlessly modern and speaks entirely of our extreme present. Imagine traveling back to Victorian England—only with vaccinations, a wad of cash, and a clean set of ruling-class garb. With Translit we get our very delicious cake, and we get to eat it, too, as we visit multiple pasts safe in the knowledge we'll get off the ride intact, in our bold new perpetual every-era/no-era. Translit's precursors are, say, *Winesburg, Ohio* and *Orlando*, and the genre's twenty-first-century tent poles are Michael Cunningham's novel *The Hours* and David Mitchell's *Cloud Atlas*. To these books we can add Hari Kunzru's gorgeous and wise *Gods without Men*.

This is Kunzru's fourth novel. It is many things, and it is certainly a reflection and an embodiment of our new world of flattened time and space. Its multiple substories span the years 1775 to 2009, and geographically cut between Manhattan, Southern California, and Iraq—or rather, a simulation of Iraq. Reading this book is not unlike watching a TV show that's simultaneously happening on multiple channels, a story filmed in different eras using differing technologies, but which taken together tell the same single story, echoing and reinfecting itself.

The core of the book concerns a prosperous young Brooklyn couple, Jaz Matharu, a second-generation Punjabi American mathematician, and Lisa, a nonobservant Jewish American who works in publishing. Jaz writes algorithms for a Wall Street firm in pre-crash 2008. He is estranged from his family in Baltimore, having broken with the Sikh way. The couple have an autistic son who turns their life upside down as they try to cope with his unexpected condition. It is not giving away too much to say that the four-year-old child, Raj, is lost during a day trip to a rock formation in the Mojave Desert near the military area of Twentynine Palms. Raj is later found, but something is different with him. He is healed, and yet … best to stop here. The book all too convincingly explores the horror of Raj's wrenching disappearance, and the catharses of his strange return.

What makes the book a Translit gem is its elegant pinballing between Jaz and Lisa's present and multiple substories that all, in some way, use a three-fingered desert rock formation called the Pinnacles as a thematic, geographic, and chronological tether—though I must add that this is not Joan Didion's desert. For Didion, the desert is a metaphor of the aridity of human relationships. For Kunzru, it is a place of God and the gods, where humans are allowed only the briefest of exposures to the power of the supernatural, and pay extreme prices in return.

In 1775, Kunzru sends an Aragonese friar, Padre Fray Francisco Garcés, on a mission into the desert, where he sees … the face of an angel? It's not quite clear, but something primal and possibly dreadful.

In 1871, a Mormon silver miner with a checkered past lies dying of mercury poisoning.

In 1920, a badly scarred linguist and his wife, caught in a passionless relationship, study what remains of a local American Indian dialect. In a moment of jealousy, the husband unleashes vengeance on his wife's Indian lover, setting off a tragic chain of events.

In 1942, the military investigates the linguist, by then a husk of a man living in a cave beneath the Pinnacles, and a cruel trick of the gods is revealed.

In 1947, a former aircraft engineer named Schmidt sets up a station at the Pinnacles to await the arrival of aliens.

In 1958, a UFO cult uses the rock formation as its energy center to make alien contact. A young girl goes missing. (I know, whenever I hear "UFO" I start making mental grocery lists, but Kunzru wisely keeps the extraterrestrial hokum to a minimum.) Ten years later, a scuzzy, Keseyesque hippie commune has taken over the Pinnacles. People come and go, damage is done, people return and some vanish.

In 2008, a peyote'd British rock star (to be played by Noel Gallagher in the movie) crashes and burns in a desert motel.

In 2008–09, a teenage Iraqi refugee has assimilated into American culture as a goth, but she works as a simulated Iraqi villager in a simulated Iraqi village used to train soldiers in assault.

Of course, none of this unfolds in chronological order—Translit!—that would be too easy and somehow not very taut. This is not a collection of stories. This is a novel. We've all read a collection of stories that seems like a novel—Alice Munro springs to mind—and yet is not a novel. But in Translit, the substories most definitely combine to make a novel. A long-form solidity emerges, even though the links between substories can be as ethereal as a snatch of music, a drug-induced sensation, a quality of light or a rock formation. The Translit author assumes the reader has the wits to connect the dots and blend the perfumes. *Gods without Men* is exemplary in this way.

A decade ago the critic James Wood used a term, "hysterical realism," to describe books of this ilk. But that somehow feels dated, as Translit prose, while crossing genres within itself, tends to be icy cool, and what once seemed like hysteria in our culture has now become a staple of daily life. The Translit reader knows there is a spirituality lacking in the modern world that can only be squeezed out of other, more authentic eras. And why not? It's all history and it's all at our fingertips. Hello, YouTube. Thank you, Wikipedia. *Oh, that Google!*

I do wonder if being a writer in 2012 means needing to be able to write in multiple genres, as do Kunzru, David Mitchell, et al., but not as some sort of postmodern party trick. It's more a statement of fact about the early twenty-first-century condition. Genre shifting is as fundamental to working with words as is punctuation and knowing the difference between serifs and sans serifs. The fact that China has recently sought to suppress time travel as a creative device for some artists (yes, it's true) makes Translit somehow subversive and highly credible.

The ultimate theme of *Gods without Men* is interconnectivity across time and space, just as interconnectedness defines the here and now. Jaz Matharu helps design a financial algorithm named Walter, and in Walter's construction, Jaz notices, "everything seemed to be linked to everything else: the net worth of retirees in Boca Raton, Fla., oscillating in harmony with the volume of cargo arriving at the port of Long Beach, Southwestern home repossessions tracking the number of avatars in the most popular online game worlds in Asia."

Indeed, Kunzru interconnects his stories—as much as needs pulling without his giving it all away. UFOs, the Angel Moroni, and German observation balloons hover in the book's skies. Children glow green, whether from the light of God or through night-vision goggles. This book strives to locate the profound amid what on the surface seems like the nothingness of the desert and the emotional sparseness of the age. It also wonders how technology connects us to our spiritual cores and where it fails. When Raj returns to his parents, he becomes the star child at the end of Stanley Kubrick's *2001*. Raj is whatever and whoever it is we all seem to have become: a race of time-traveling time-killers Googling and Wikiing until our machines transform into something smarter than ourselves, we humans left only to hope the machines may save us in the process.

Sometimes if you stare at a word long enough, or say it too many times, the word disintegrates in your head and a new meaning emerges. "British," as in British Columbia, is one such word. After a lifetime spent here, it's only now that I look at this word and think to myself, *British, British, British, British, British, British, British … Britishbritis hbritishbritish* … B   r   i t   i   s   h.

Hmmm … I've never given the word so much consideration until this moment. And now suddenly it's stopped being a word and has turned into a sound effect, like the noise made by rotating scrubbers in a car wash: britishbritishbritish…

And then suddenly it turns into a word again: British. The Queen, the Sex Pistols. Oh, yeah, that's right, those people colonized this place.

I get to thinking that to outsiders, a name like British Columbia must look colonial or exotic or throwbacky or, at the very least, a word that implies interesting souvenir shops. Tea anyone?

I grew up in Vancouver, graduating from high school in 1979 in a suburb called the British Properties. It's those houses you see on the mountain slope to the north, marching up the slope to the 600-foot line. These days the British Properties are Beverly Hills with spruce trees, but in the 1970s it was pure *Brady Bunch*—dead center of the middle class.

The British Properties is Vancouver's equivalent to selling Manhattan for twenty-four dollars. In 1932, England's Guinness family bought its 1,600 acres for $50 per acre. Then they created a mountain subdivision by building a network of roads throughout the easternmost parcel of land. Many of the old logging roads were repurposed as suburban drives and lanes. The Guinness family then promptly named these after friends, relatives, nannies, country estates, and pets. I believe the street I grew up on was named after their Labrador's kennel.

But then suddenly.

But then suddenly … wait … what's going on here? Suddenly I've just been ripped away from the present and I'm flown back into the past, back into a noontime group of freezing-cold soaking-wet loggers. It's April of 1911 and they're cussing beside a Capilano Valley ravine. They're cussing because the flume downstream has popped a plank and can't be fixed until sundown, and this means a day spent idling with no pay and the only deck of cards to be had is missing two jacks. Who wants to go into the city tonight to find a woman or two? Depends on the ferry. Depends on the weather. Where the hell are the horses and lunch? Christ, I'm so sick of the smell of burning slash and I think my chink launderer's got some laudanum that'll land you on cloud nine.

And then, whaam! Suddenly I jump ahead to six decades later and an eight-year-old version of me in the back seat of a Ford Fairlane convertible purring up Stevens Drive at forty-five miles per hour. I'm returning home from an appendectomy. I look out the window: down the ravine and below to the east I can see the tiniest fragment of an old railway flume below the road, a brutal fir-log structure now decomposing, almost completely devoured by time and the forest that replaced the one stripped away. The bridge is a 3-D nurse log sprouting salal and huckleberries, and a young me has trouble believing that the bridge even exists in the first place.

"What are you thinking about in the back seat?" It's my mother.

"Nothing." But of course I'm thinking furiously about the bridge, wondering how it can exist because I know as a fact that our suburb was hacked away from what was once a first-growth rain forest—first there was a total absence of history and then there was ... history: me, my family, the Fairlane, television, and Jell-O. I don't want to think that there was some intermediate layer of history between the primordial and me. I don't want the flume to exist; yet it does.

And suddenly I, you, me, we are in the year 2010. It's February and I'm across the river in a gondola headed up Grouse Mountain, I'm looking down on Stevens Drive, now a few miles away across the reservoir, the dam, and river below. I'm with three German journalists, showing them the city, but I'm burning out from host fatigue and the Winter Olympics. I'm looking at Stevens Drive and thinking about the meth lab they found in the 400 block three years back, a kidney-shaped swimming pool turned acid green, filled with leftover meth-making chemicals and the feathers of ducks stupid enough to land in it. I'm thinking of the house just off Stevens Drive's west edge that in 1966 sold for $59,000, and that just sold to an offshore buyer for $4.5 million. I'm looking at the chain-link fence that separated where I grew up from the Capilano River watershed, on the other side of which is second-growth forest that merges into first-growth forest, which then continues pretty much unmolested, right up to the Arctic Circle, over the Arctic Ocean, and into Siberia before any further evidence of humanity is to be found.

"Dawgluss," says one of the reporters. "Can you please show me where it was that you grew up." So I do. The reporter looks to the speck beside the chain-link fence and does a small double take—he can see that there's nothing but wilderness for thousands of miles on the other side of that fence. "Oh. I see. When you wrote about growing up on the other side of a fence from the wilderness, I thought you were just being metaphorical. But you weren't."

No, I wasn't.

And then suddenly it's August 25, 1546, and I'm in a huckleberry grove overlooking the eastern Capilano Canyon bathed in hot yellow sun. Leonardo da Vinci has just finished his last brush stroke on La Giaconda, and I'm watching a young mother from the Skwxwú7mesh (Squamish) Nation picking blue huckleberries on a hot afternoon with a child strapped to her shoulders. It's been a good berry year: good and regular snow, rain, and sun. It's sunny and hot in a way that the valley only ever is for one moon cycle a year, but the young mother's stomach is cramping and she's wondering if she'll be able to scramble down the path to the ocean by sundown, and whether her stomach will mend. The pains are sharp. Then, through a hole in the forest caused by a tree downed by lightning, this young woman thinks she sees a glint of something shiny floating up the side of Grouse Mountain. She rubs her eyes and shakes her head and looks again—just her eyes playing tricks on her. She returns to her berries.

And suddenly, whaam! I'm in a small drawing room in London, England, and it's 1925 and night-time and pissing rain out and inside five men in suits from Jermyn Street are at the tail end of two bottles of claret and several cigars. They have pens and in front of them is a map of what looks almost like golf greens, except that the shapes define roads. These men are wasted. They're cackling with glee. One of them has tuberculosis and doesn't know it. A piece of lung lands on the map and he wipes it away and writes down, "Barnham. That's the name of the kennel I was at last week. Damn good place. Feed their dogs damn well, but I can't say that 'bout the Micks they keep out back." More cackles. A street 3,000 miles away is named.

The shifts continue.

Now we're in a de Havilland Beaver single-prop flight over Atlin, BC. It's July 1978 and my father is flying to Kluane National Park with my younger brother and me. My father is thinking of how he put himself through med school flying fighter jets for the Canadian Air Force. He's thinking of the years he spent flying over Cold War Germany where two of his children were born—instant mutually assured destruction—and now he's thinking of how free he feels flying over northern BC in his own plane during an era of supreme peace, when the land still remains, even in 1978, largely unexplored, where the weather can change in ninety seconds. It is all he ever wanted, this sense of freedom, this sense of everything still being possible, this sense of the power of the present to always overwrite the past.

I'm looking out from inside the Beaver. This isn't where I wanted to be that weekend. This is never where I wanted to be any weekend, dragged out into the hinterlands, forced to see landscapes of unutterable beauty—places without malls or names or any anything, just this relentless blankness that barely has any existence on maps. And what's driving me onward that afternoon in the Beaver is gold. Specifically, my younger brother and I are going to pan for gold when we land. We've brought gold pans and paperbacks on the subject, and now consider ourselves experts. But the noise, the noise! Have you ever flown in a Beaver? The otherworldly views beneath the plane, utterly wasted on impatient teens: the jade-colored Pacific waters when we were fueling up on the coast at Oona River; shrimp floating in the dockwater as though locked in amber; a hailstorm almost eats the plane thirty miles north of Hazelton; a flock of canvasbacks flying toward a mountain slope as though back into time. I think to myself, if this plane went down in thirty seconds, could the authorities ever locate us? Black-box technology is still primitive.

Cut to …

Cut to roughly 8:05 p.m. on the evening of April 28, 1947: a twin-engine Trans Canada Airline Lodestar 10,000 feet above sea level carrying twelve passengers and three crew members from Lethbridge to Vancouver experiences a small engine explosion. It rocks the plane. The flight attendants make a face at each other and quickly gather what coffee service that remains. Within a minute their plane and its passengers are debris on the side of Mount Elsay, four miles north of Deep Cove, British Columbia, a twenty-five-minute drive to downtown Vancouver. In the futile search for the craft shortly after this plane's disappearance, dozens of leads are followed, including one from Mrs. E. Van Welter of Mayne Island, BC, who found a photo of a woman in the belly of a salmon she was cleaning. But the plane is never found, not for five decades. In 1997, fifteen skeletons are accidentally discovered by municipal workers. The plane went down perfectly vertically.

Cut to…

Cut to me accidentally walking into an RCMP-detection-proof pot ranch in the Nelson Mountains circa 2004, wondering whether this intrusion merits being shot by unseen weapons. I freeze. I walk backward slowly. You don't mess with this shit. I get away.

Cut to February 2006: getting sunburned in Haida Gwaii collecting sea sponges on the beach off of Towhill Road. In the span of three hours I experience five different weather systems.

Cut to 2011: attending the Chinese/Anglo super-wedding of friends in Richmond, getting lost in the suburb's memory-dissolving street grid, finally arriving to a seafood emporium beside a monorail, palm trees, and dollar stores, expecting to meet nobody, instead meeting five people I didn't know would be there. Dinner topics include Canadian security in Afghanistan and the safety of flying south across the Sierra Nevada Mountains in January or February.

It's now as if we're dissolving into the province itself, like sugar into tea. Hippie children with blank blue eyes surfing off the Tofino coast in the middle of February. A Japanese family in 1942 being issued prison garb and shown the World War II internment camp where they will spend the war years, in Kaslo, stripped of everything they own, all to be auctioned off to friends of friends of the law. Forty-six years later their daughter will marry my brother. They will live on Zero Avenue, across the street from the United States border. During an August barbecue they will watch a group of thirty Eastern European-looking people with backpacks and terrified faces run up the street, up toward the city.

Time is speeding up. Time is slowing down. There's nothing to measure time against in this land, so recently taken by man. No, that's not true, there are seasons. There are weather patterns. *Look*: it's me, walking to school down the Baden Powell Trail, from kindergarten to seventh grade, and every year by October 15 the snow is at the middle tower of the Grouse Mountain gondola.

Cut to 2012: sometimes it takes until December until the middle tower gets snow. Time seems to be breaking or bending. What year is it? What happens to the Squamish mother and her child? Does she make it by nightfall? (She does.) What happens to everyone?

The year is 2057. Vancouver is now a city-state with full recognition from the United Nations. Its population is 4.7 million people. Vancouver Island is its own Canadian province. Canada still exists. The oil country up north merged with Alberta two decades ago. What was once south-central Western BC is still a dead zone from the 2026 explosions at Hanford—a shame the wind was going north that day. It was a Thursday and nobody knew what to do except watch the satellite scans.

And I'm dead.

And you're dead.

It's the way things go, and yet British Columbia still hasn't become whatever it's ultimately going to be. It was born too late. It never got finalized. Unlike the rest of the new world, it just squeaked by under the radar, and its landscape is too hard to tame. Utopian communities came and went. The copper came and went, and so did the natural gas, but the people went on and will always go on. Because they like it that way, and because life, like the land, is wild.

Britishbritishbritishbritish.

Oh, stop flapping your lips. We have lives to lead.

In a few days I turn fifty and my e-mail inbox is starting to ping with requests for quick interviews hanging on the hook, "Gen X Turns Fifty." There's a part of me that always knew this day might come—and may come again at sixty and seventy. But what I only ever really wanted from the media age-wise, and what I never got, was to be included in one of those essentially cheesy "Twenty in Their Twenties" articles that are stock in trade or lifestyle magazines. I know, but it's what I really wanted, and unfortunately when I finally did something that might make me worthy of a "Twenty in Their Twenties" article, it was too late: *Generation X* was published two months after my thirtieth birthday on March 1, 1991; I had to live with the fact that magazines don't run articles on "Thirty in Their Thirties." By your thirties you should be doing whatever it is you're supposed to be doing with your life and just get on with it—which is what I suppose happened with me as much as to anyone else.

1991 was more than twenty years ago—and this was before not only the Internet but also e-mail. I remember worrying about my phone bill each month. And I remember the Kuwait War and I remember the end of the existence of the USSR; I remember the snow on the ground during that particularly mild winter in Montreal where I was living at the time of *Generation X*'s publication. I also remember waiting for the first copy of the book to arrive. Ask any writer: the true moment of birth is when the FedEx envelope is ripped open and a book is fully midwifed into the world.

Here are a few *Generation X* facts: it was originally going to be called *52 Daffodils* after a story contained within the book. I wonder what life would be like now if I'd done that. My Canadian publisher also declined to publish the book, which forever gave American publishers right of first refusal on new books, and which began the myth within the Canadian writing world that I was trying to be American not Canadian. But it took years for me to figure out what was actually happening—there was no Internet to crystalize trends on a dime: trends took place across the span of years, not days. Trends had backlashes and then counter-backlashes that also went on for years. These days a meme is good for a few days or a few weeks, max.

So, back to March of 1991, and waiting for the book to arrive. It finally did, but not by FedEx; rather, it arrived via a subcontracted delivery agency that was several weeks late and dropped two books off at the door with a big gash along their top edges. The covers of the books also had folded flaps, except the machine that did the folding goofed and the pages of the book stuck out a half inch and looked ridiculous. All in all you couldn't have asked for a more depressing book birth. I phoned my editor in New York and he knew exactly how bad the binding and printing was, and he did that thing people do when they know they've done something wrong, which is to say, he turned it around and got mad at me for being so picky.

So that was March of 1991. The 1980s were over and I had this sadness that some dimension of history, a certain kind of potency, was over; that somehow as a culture we'd reached a point where we couldn't count on decades to create looks and feels and tones the way the '60s, '70s, or '80s did. I think it's called pattern fatigue. Meanwhile, Francis Fukuyama was declaring the end of history. The art world was dead. Life felt stagnant.

And then grunge happened.

And then the Internet arrived.

And then the decade began generating, for lack of a better word, decade-osity. The '90s felt like the '90s in a real and good way. Through a stroke of good fate, the same editor, who tried to downplay the book's botched first printing, *did* have the foresight to choose the name *Generation X* from the list of alternates to *52 Daffodils*. And because of this, the years 1991 to 2000 were far more action-packed than they were in some other parallel universe with a different title.

There was a lot of absurd stuff that went on during that decade. I think most everyone remembers the endless articles on the concept of "Generation X": What *is* it? Who *are* they? Does Generation X even *exist*? If so, how can we make *money* from it? Are they boomers or are they different? Do they require a different management style?

And on and on.

I've never had an answer to any of these questions, although, as a shorthand, I said, and continue to say, that if you liked the Talking Heads "back in the day," then you're probably X. Or, if you liked New Order. Or Joy Division. Or something, *anything*, other than that wretched Forrest Gumpy baby-boomer we-run-the-planety crap that boomers endlessly yammer on about. I mean, good for them, have and enjoy your generation—but please don't tell me that that's me, too, because it's not, it never was, and it never will be. The whole point of Gen X was, and continues to be, a negation of being forced into baby boomerdom against one's will.

And of course there's—*sigh*—Generation Y, or, rather, Gen Y, which is much more loveable than Generation X because Gen Y's parents are those Forrest Gumpy baby-boomery people, and cheerfully for them, Gen Y acts as their mirror and shadow, thus offering them a bonus extra channel through which they can discuss and view themselves. In a demographic sense, Gen Y really is a generation, while X is only a psychographic.

Do you like the Talking Heads, yes or no?

I remember writing the book. I began in November of 1989. In a fit of authorial romance, I used a tiny advance, $22,500, and took out a lease on a small bungalow in Palm Springs (I know, I just used the word bungalow in a sentence) that I regretted the moment I arrived. Palm Springs wasn't anything in 1989. It wasn't midcentury modern, it wasn't Coachella Valley Music and Arts Festival, it wasn't gay, and it wasn't trendy, groovy, hip, or anything else. It was a sci-fi-like world where an invisible glass dome landed atop a luxury community a week before Richard Nixon's resignation, and I was one of the first explorers to be allowed back into the place after the dome's removal. This was a coincidence. I just thought Palm Springs would be a cheap, pleasant (and yes, romantic) place to write a novel. I didn't realize until I got there how it was an embodiment of a long-outdated way of viewing the world, one where the acme of existence was to ride shotgun in Bob Hope's golf cart, or to sniff the swimming pool chlorine off of Kim Novak's neck. I was the only person under the age of fifty-five who wasn't working in a hospital or a hotel, and even at that, people my age were scarce. There were only two delis where you could buy a coffee (as if coffee availability is a measure of anything), but it was in this fantasmagorically unhip kingdom where I was stuck because I was locked into a lease in the state of California, and to break that lease would be credit suicide. So during very lonely days I drove around the highways and dead subdivisions, and golf courses, and secluded desert shotgun-practice sites in my Volkswagen Type-3 fastback that had neither an air conditioner nor a stereo—and I used a battery-powered cassette recorder and played the Stone Roses or Morrissey or usually British bands who felt like they were speaking to me from another galaxy.

While I was writing the book, I thought there would be, at most, a few people who I attended school with in Vancouver, who might kind of get what I was writing about—or maybe a few people down in Seattle, which was a little bit like Vancouver back then. I was surprised and remain surprised to this day that so many people clicked with X—or with any of the books I've written—because it always seems, in the end, that writing is such a desolate, lonely profession and it never gets less lonely. In fact, as I sit here a few days before turning fifty, it feels so lonely that I wonder if I can visit the place of writing anymore, which, in a backward way, tells me that's exactly why I should go forward. The things worth writing about, and the things worth reading about, are the things that feel almost beyond description at the start and are, because of that, frightening.

Everybody on Earth Is Feeling
the Exact Same Thing as You:
Notes on Relationships
in the Twenty-First Century

1. It's very hard to imagine calling someone
   and saying, "Hey, come over to my house
   and we'll sit next to each other on chairs
   and go online together!" Going online
   is such an intrinsically solitary act and
   yet, ironically, it allows for groups to
   be formed.

2. I think it's very funny the way even the most nice-seeming people turn into trolls and monsters when they go online alone at night. Anonymity unmasks them.

3. Last year at a conference about cities I met this guy from Google who asked me what I knew about Fort McMurray, Alberta. I told him it's an oil-extraction town in the middle of nowhere, and because of this, it has the most disproportionately male demographic of any city in North America. Its population is maybe 50,000. I asked him why he was asking and he said, "Because it has the highest per capita video streaming rate of anywhere in North America."

4. Dutch researchers doing a survey of the effects of pornography on men had to cancel the study because they simply couldn't find a man anywhere on Earth who hadn't, at some point, sought out porn. They were trying to find an "uncontaminated" statistical control pool and had to abandon their project.

5. I don't know if women go online looking for porn. It's hard to imagine them doing that. They must think men are pigs. But they must do something, even if it's just a fantasy of making it with the tradesman who installed the new stove.

6. I think that because of the Internet, straight people are now having the same amount of sex as gay guys are always supposed to be having. There's a weird hollowed-out look I can see on the face of people who are getting too much sex delivered to them via the Internet—or anywhere else, for that matter. They've gotten laid but there's a whiff of failure to it all. Is this it? I find that younger people of all types are highly aware that too much sex will desensitize them to love. In the old days they never had that option. So that's totally new.

7. On the old *Mary Tyler Moore Show*, Lou Grant asked Mary how many times a girl could be with a different

man before she became "that kind of girl," and Mary thought about it very carefully and said, "Six." Some psychologists have come to the conclusion that most people have five or six "loves" and once they use them up, that's it. Sixes get used up very quickly in the new information world.

8. People in the pornography industry have found that the magic price point for people subscribing to a porn site is $29.95. The moment you cross that line, potential customers balk and leave. This is called the "porn wall," and it seems to be an impenetrable thing—a constant that's built into us by nature, like the nesting instinct of birds or the molecular weight of zinc.

9. In the 1990s there was a thirty-year-old Latino guy who passed himself off as a hot teenage girl in a Florida high school and spent a year and a half there before they found out. I think he attended his PTA meetings as his own father. I think that in certain ways, we've all become Latino guys pretending to be hot cheerleaders—except maybe you're not pretending to be a cheerleader, you're pretending to be a studly cowboy or whoever it is you wish you could be to the person on the other end who has no way of disproving it.

10. Sometimes people really connect online, but, of course, they live far away from each other. So, ultimately, one of them buys a plane ticket and flies across the country to meet the other in person. If there's no physical chemistry it leads to one very depressing drink and some desultory conversation before they both go home. People in the dating industry call these people "next-flight-homers." Sometimes people really connect online and when they meet in person they physically click. People in the dating industry call them "room-getters."

11. I sometimes wonder about people who wake up and spend almost the whole day online. When they go to bed at night, they'll have almost no organic memories of their own. If they do this for a long time, you can

begin to say that their intelligence is, in a true sense, artificial. Which I guess means sex lives have never been as artificial as they are now.

12. People seem to be pickier about bodies these days. New high-definition TV cameras have changed the way we look at bodies. Even a faint acne scar looks like the Grand Canyon on a high-def screen. TV casting agents have started to heavily favor actors with perfectly smooth skin. It's like the dermatological equivalent of the introduction of sound into film in 1929.

13. It's more pressure than ever for movie stars to look and be a certain way, and it's hard growing old in the modern world. It's hard to imagine Jack Nicholson with Alzheimer's. David Bowie is going to be seventy soon. I don't know how I feel about all of this. At least online you can fake youth—you can fake everything.

14. It's only when you don't have an Internet connection or lose your phone that you realize how alone you are in the world. I don't know if I'd want to go back to being 1992 me, or 1982 me—all that time I spent being largely isolated and alienated.

15. I don't think people being on their devices all the time is an indicator of social isolation. Maybe it's the opposite. In Manhattan about one person in three on any given sidewalk is using a wireless device. Some people say that's bad because they're not "in the moment," but I think it's kind of nice because you have visible proof that people need and want to be with other people.

16. I watched *Looking for Mr. Goodbar* a few weeks ago. It was Richard Gere and Diane Keaton in 1970s New York and I was horrified by how low-tech it was back then. It's like people lived in badly furnished caves connected by landlines. It was a real eye-opener.

17. Once you get used to a certain level of connection, there's just no way to go back to where you were

before. The thing about 2012 is that people are more connected than they've ever been before—except they've been tricked into thinking they're more isolated than ever. How did that happen?

18. I find that whenever I stay with people, the first ninety minutes of the day are spent online collectively waking up the way we used to wake up with newspapers. Every morning when I open my e-mails, there's a part of me that feels like I'm scratching a lottery ticket, except instead of just winning things, you can also lose things, too. Money. Friends. Status. Work. Love. It's the best moment in the day for many people—that delicious three-second window when, after reading all your papers and blogs, you say, "Ahhhh ... now I'm going to check my personal e-mail." Because it's all about you.

Growing up, whenever I thought of what
the future might look like, the image that
always came to mind was of a jet ramp
you'd walk onto at a Chinese airport
after a long flight on a budget airline.
No windows, and the air would be hot,
muggy, and smell of farts and engines,
and there'd be backlit advertisements
for obscure banking services and uni-
dentifiable, scary-looking foods—huge
tureens filled with things like cooked
baby birds and donkey gonads, genetic
broth to be consumed only at one's peril.
On the ground, instead of litter, there'd
be items people had abandoned: frayed
luggage, dead phone cards, ice cream
turned to cheese in the heat, oil-soiled
garments. The ramp would go on and on,
and there'd never be an airline terminal,
just this endless heat and claustrophobia
and sense of environmental depletion.

I actually *do* find a bit of that in China, mostly when I stray 100 yards or so off the metropolitan showcase arteries. But what I find on a larger scale is an overpowering sense of damaged brilliance: the morning white light off the shimmering East China Sea turning Shanghai's sky into a massive magnifying lens made of burning coal and vaporized cash. Through this lens are apartment buildings that continue uninterrupted as they recede over the earth's curvature, and skyscrapers shaped like Transformers, emerging like gods from the mists below them, quietly overseeing traffic jams that can linger for months. These towers will make magnificent ruins. At their feet also exists a different type of Chinese road: empty roads in tranquil economic development zones, seamlessly paved, lovingly landscaped and tweezed, connecting to homes for foreigners and the local oligarchy. This would be Shanghai's Pudong neighborhood—or, as the expats there call it, "Pu Jersey"—on the south shore of the Huangpu River.

In my hotel, I take the elevator downstairs to meet my tour guide. In the mezzanine, I walk through a consumer fantasia mall entirely devoid of customers. Its three sleek silent floors are filled with surprisingly well-branded boutiques—Lego, Moleskine, and Muji—as well as those selling the finest French and Chilean wines. When I do see people, it's near the hotel's entrance: expats with laptops savoring that most delectable of all luxuries in China, Wi-Fi connected to a Hong Kong server, bypassing the notorious Great Firewall of China, allowing users to access Google, Twitter, and Facebook. Were these data parasites to be using a Chinese server, and were they to ask Google a question, their request would take a strangely long time to go through. Instead of .25 seconds, ten seconds might pass; that is, if an answer were to come at all. I've been told there are buildings the size of airports filled with bureaucrats who personally inspect all Google searches. Over the next few days I ask most people I meet, locals and foreigners, whether this is true, and nobody knows for sure, but there's just enough hesitation in people's eyes to make me think this isn't just an urban legend, because Google searches simply don't take ten or more seconds. I wonder what it must be like to see all of the things people search for on Google. You'd be unshockable or, worse, you'd be utterly bored of human beings—you'd know our limits and our extremes. Which makes me wonder what's going to happen when the Internet finally does become sentient; is this newly born super-entity, the Singularity, going to be our chummy new best friend, or is it going to blink its metaphorical eyes, take one look at us all, and say, "You know what? I've got better things to do than service all you idiots. I'm *outta* here," and then promptly pull the plug on itself?

Shanghai is where the communications conglomerate Alcatel-Lucent makes the routing and switching equipment that moves data through its optical-fiber pathways. I arrive at their Chinese branch after a five-minute drive down a road built in the early 1980s—that is, when this section of Pudong was selected to be an industrial development zone. Alcatel-Lucent Shanghai Bell (called ASB) is a showcase of China's move from relative isolation into the larger world. In the 1990s its foreign revenues were 5 percent of sales. This year they were 50 percent. ASB is one of four big players in the telecommunications industry in China, along with Nokia, Siemens, and China's Huawei and ZTE. Globally, one would add to this list Juniper Networks, Ericsson, and Cisco Systems. There really aren't that many firms who make the complicated routers and switching equipment needed to handle the speed and numbers required by our current society—the numbers in China are certainly humbling. There are 1.3 billion people (three United States), and 600 million of these people currently have mobile phones. By 2015 the government wants everyone in large cities to have 100 megabytes per second of data speed, people in secondary cities to have 20 megabytes, and all other citizens to have 4. In a slightly longer time frame, it is widely assumed that the ideological bulldozer known as the next Five-Year Plan, slated to begin shortly, will give every Chinese citizen 100 megabytes per second. That's every episode of *The Simpsons* ever made downloadable in a few seconds—or the entire NASA space program circa 1974.

Who knows what this speed will do to a society. Can we know? Can we predict? One might look to Google for the answer—Google being the only entity on earth that has its act together as much as China, but even Google doesn't know what happens when you give large numbers of people a large amount of speed. To this end, Google is currently wiring Kansas City to give all residents one *giga*byte per second of data because they're curious to find out.

Who would have foreseen search engines, Twitter, or lolcats.com from the early version of the Internet? And who know what lies in wait for the Internet's next Great Leap Forward?

1

I find myself in a seven-story early 1980s building whose style is defined by off-white stucco, peach-toned highlights, missing lightbulbs, and benign neglect. It's like a sun-bleached spread from *Domus* the week after the implosion of Memphis. I'm getting déjà vu within déjà vu—the same sense of creeping recognition I get when I fly too much, land in too many airports, and realize that being able to go anywhere you want, whether online or in a plane, can actually feel the same as going nowhere.

I'm taken to a first-floor display center, an art form as perfected by the Chinese as Ming vases and terra-cotta warriors. This center is a model home of tomorrow, which, I'm told by two well-rehearsed and confident male tour guides, offers "a converged IT experience. Interactivity driving the delivery of the right message to the right people." In my mind I revert to elementary school and put on my highly worthy field-trip face.

The rooms in the house of tomorrow are well designed—like display suites in a premium condominium development targeted at Russians. The furniture is far better than what most people have anywhere on Earth these days, yet it shares one thing in common with most things everywhere: it was all made in China. Noting this, of course, triggers that butterfly-in-the-stomach feeling we all get when we wonder when China is going to—well, let's just say it—economically crash and burn. It has to happen sometime. Maybe it will plateau and never crash, but that's not mathematically possible, so... The worry about some sort of bursting bubble is as palpable in the air as the smell of grilled meat and low-sulfur coal.

In China, with its in-your-face sense of sheer numbers, you quickly realize how plausibly secondary the United States and Europe are becoming on the global scene. A sales executive I spoke with in an airport lounge a few weeks back told me that in US high schools, they show you a map of the world and ask you to locate France. If you even point to Europe, then you get your high-school diploma. In China, you have to identify all the *arrondissements* of Paris and give a highly technical analysis of the paper fibers used in the map, as well as an analysis of the toxicity of the inks used to print it.

The television in the home of tomorrow is displaying the finale of *American Idol*, season seven, which I'd actually like to sit and watch ("And the winner of American Idol *is* ..."). I start to tune out the statistics I'm being told about the future of China's consumers, which largely have to do with Chinese advertisers targeting the right Chinese consumers. This is depressing, and one would hope China might do something different with targeted data than just nurture shopping—possibly something gruesome and eye opening, but different nonetheless. Seated on a comfy leather sofa, watching the end of a reality series, I muse on the 7 billion people on earth, and how almost everybody these days voraciously devours countless unbundled fragments of our creative past, either by watching it as a YouTube clip or by sticking it in a plastic envelope for sale on eBay, and how we seem to be consuming far more culture than we create. I'm wondering if everything before 2001 will be considered the Age of Content, and all the time thereafter as the Age of Devouring.

2

I head up to the third floor to meet Dr. Xing Gue, Vice President of Offshore Production. Xing began as an engineer. His English is flawless, and he discusses a recent trip to Holland to negotiate a deal with a telecommunications partner there. During the course of his negotiations, he found himself thinking, "We add one Holland worth of customers a *month* onto China."

I ask Dr. Xing what surprises him most about the new China versus the old China, and he says, "Golf. I never thought I'd see a golf course in China. And now it's a huge thing. BMW is having a masters tournament in Shanghai this October."

This isn't an answer I might have expected, but that's why we ask questions. As sustainability is on my mind, I ask Dr. Xing if the present pace of Chinese development is sustainable. He smiles and says, "My daughter is nine, and she said to me, 'Can you fold a piece of paper over fifty times? No. It would be 1,200 miles thick.'" There is a pause.

So there's my answer—I think.

I ask about the most likely next new technologies, and he says, "In the future your mobile phone will be making many calls all at once rather than just one. You probably won't know about many of them." He's referring to things like GPS and all of the secondary data our phones transmit: who we're calling; when we call them; our call patterns; the tone of our voices; trigger words such as "I feel like pizza," and Lord only knows what else we unwittingly spew out into the world. "Machine-to-machine communication is absolutely the future of speed, profit, capacity, and bandwidth maximization." Everything about his tone leaves me with no doubt that this is the true and correct future. Xing adds, "China has a cloud network of 600 million users, and all of these phones will eat up a huge amount of energy. Something must be done to reduce this." He mentions his company's plan for a genuine thousand-fold energy reduction in data processing. The Chinese recognition of the need to be green is actually a strong recurring theme during my time here. People at all levels of society realize that greening needs to be done and that it is inevitable. The only problem is that it's difficult, expensive, and unprofitable to implement—which is why it doesn't happen very much anywhere, let alone in China.

A slight earthquake jiggles the building and it is brushed off as though it were a mosquito passing through. In China the notion of things being "cool" doesn't really exist, but it is certainly uncool to comment on earthquakes. The Japanese earthquake was barely a month before this visit.

We discuss the work done by ASB's research facility, which is a patent-generating machine: 6,400 patents since 2002 from just over 100 researchers. With some pride Xing says, "In the past, ideas and technologies were a one-way street into China, but the number of patents generated by Shanghai now equals those from Alcatel's US division."

Xing adds, "We have a committee that determines what goes to patent. Patents must be global and good for business." When asked about the amount of basic research done in China, Xing says, "Any project development time that might go beyond two years is iffy. We are an industrial research lab, and we can feel the breath of our competitors on our necks."

Xing's seeming casualness about the absence of basic or fundamental research is unusual in the industry and is probably just a brave face put on for nosy visitors. With so much competition, most companies are running as fast as they can just to stay in the same place, let alone go forward. But without some fundamental new way of manipulating the universe that might be discovered with pure research, new technological development will hit the wall. And this might be a good thing. Haven't we all wanted to take a year or two off to digest the technologies we already have?

Before I leave Dr. Xing's office, I comment on the number of young people in the Shanghai branch, and he explains that when creating research teams, the company likes to mix young staff with old—to "break patterns."

At what point in Chinese history you were born is pivotal in determining your sensibility. If the Western world had the whole Generation X and Y experience, mainland China has what it calls "Born in the '80s" or the "Post-'80s." These are 240 million adults born after the government's implementation of the one-child policy. As a group, their upbringing has been so different from that of their parents that, within China, one generation looks at the other more as another species than as a different generation. Everything about their existence is different from those of the Mao Zedong era: liberalized politics, a higher quality of education, nonexistent sibling relationships (and the Napoleonic sense of entitlement that comes from that), but mostly technology—computers, the Internet, and mobile phones. If one ever needs proof that technology rewires the human brain, simply speak to anyone in China older than fifty. And if one starts to look at the Post-'90s, one finds an even newer group of people already different from those a decade ahead of them, a group being demonized simply for being alive and for not having had to endure the hardships endured by their predecessors. *Plus ça change…*

I ask Dr. Xing how his paper-folding daughter is different from him and his generation, and he tells me, "My daughter challenges everything I say. She's of the newest generation, and her school is ultra-democratic. It used to be that the teachers selected which students would receive awards. Now the students elect the winners." Once again, not the answer I might have expected.

3

I get into a small, muggy elevator to head to another floor. The door opens onto two floors that are entirely blacked out and sleepwalky people enter and leave as though navigating the capsized *SS Poseidon*. I disembark on the sixth floor, where I find groups of tiny little old ladies moving pots around, wiping banisters with rags, and catnapping in conference rooms mothballed since the great telecom crash. It's hard to imagine the cosmopolitan young women strolling about the Bund, armed with MasterCards and a hunter-gatherer gleam in their eyes, ever seeing themselves as these small, bustling women forty years down the road.

I then have a short conversation with Mr. Yong Wang, Director of Asian Region Recruiting. Athletic and alert, he's the son of a teacher from a small city 200 miles from Shanghai. Wang joined ASB in 2001, and when I speak of the generational discussion I've just had, he tells me, "Old and young are different species in China. I am a child of the children of the Cultural Revolution. I was born in 1974. I believe in changing real life pragmatically"— as opposed to relying on dogma and cant. "People born in the '80s are different again from people like myself."

I ask Mr. Wang, "Aside from your generation, what *class* would you consider yourself." He doesn't understand the question. I say, "In North America, if you ask someone what class they're in, almost all will say middle class, regardless of income. Would you consider yourself middle class?" Our conversation dies. In fact, I ask this question of pretty much everyone I meet in China, and not one person has a ready answer—these days one can't really say one is a member of the people's revolution—so how *can* one label oneself? The answer appears to be not at all. China is adrift on a classless sea. One can't help but see and hear tales of increased prosperity in China since 1990, yet the future inhabitants of those dream condos displayed in the lobby, currently age fifteen, are without class labels. Wang finally says, "Perhaps we are aspirationally middle class."

What impresses me about his answer is that Wang is from a small city south of Shanghai whose second language is English, and he uses the word "aspirationally" with ease. (I also note, during my time in China, that nobody peppers his or her English with the word "like," which is pleasant. And whenever Chinese English starts to sound a bit robotic, I realize that can stem from the absence of junk words such as "umm" and "uh" and "really." Just saying.)

4

Lunch is next—at a nearby restaurant that one might find in an upscale strip mall in Tampa, Florida. I am with Paul Ross, a US expat Buddhist and head of the Asian Marketing Division, who tells me that China is becoming, if not middle class, "then certainly more bourgeois. It's subtle things, like ATM machines or owning dogs as pets. Or the reemergence of formal pronouns for 'you' in daily conversation, similar to the use of *vous* instead of *tu* in French. By changing that one pronoun, you undo the PC dogma of the cultural revolution. People are acknowledging that theirs is no longer a classless society."

I ask what this says about the direction of Chinese society as a whole, and his answer surprises me: "You never hear people ask a European, 'What is your country going to be doing in twenty years?' One assumes that the French will still be busy being French, and the Norwegians will still be busy being Norwegian. So when you ask a European what they'll be doing in two decades, you're basically asking them what it means to be alive. And yet with China, the question of the future is all anyone asks, which is fine, but the question is loaded because you're discussing both what it means to be Chinese *and* what it means to be alive."

Indeed, Norway is not being convulsed with massive internal migration while skipping over several generations of technology at once, making the country a living laboratory that shows the rest of the world what the future might hold for us. China really does make me wonder, *what is it we're learning about ourselves from all of this new technology that we didn't already know?* As mentioned earlier, some people believe that the Internet now occupies the slots in your brain once occupied by politics and religion. Perhaps this is the finishing line that China is beating us to.

The bill arrives and Paul scratches the bottom of the receipt. I ask him why, and he says, "A few years back, nobody was giving or keeping receipts for anything, so the government came up with the idea of putting scratch-and-win prizes on the bottom of all receipts. Now everybody keeps every receipt. It worked." Human nature.

On the way out the door I ask Paul what he thinks of the whole "Born in the '80s/'90s" thing. He says, "These days, young people will now stay at home on the weekend, doing nothing, like people do anywhere. They view that as freedom. To put a finer point on it, the way you perceive your own freedom *is* your freedom."

As I get into the car to drive back to the ASB factory, I'm thinking about freedom—the freedom to think or do whatever one chooses to do, or not do. It would seem China, as with so many other things, is now developing a middle-class sense of leisure time. What *are* the implications of supersaturating a formerly agrarian society with massive doses of 3G and 4G technologies? How does that affect one's sense of self? One's sense of being a member of society? Westerners have a very sentimental sense of the self. People who came of age in the twentieth century most likely grew up with a sense of the noble individual— the literary sense of self discussed earlier, the sense of self in which one sees one's life as a story, a grand narrative. For an ego created in this system, the assault on the self that is triggered by the Internet is extreme.

One is no longer an individual; one is now merely one unit among seven billion other units. Emotionally, for Westerners, it is a great step down. But for the Chinese, to go online and to use a mobile device is a huge step up; instead of being numberless, one is now an individual within a globe of fellow individuals. Let's vote! Let's shop! Let's post pictures of our new puppy! *LOL!*

ASB's router factory, one of several in China, is located just across Ningqiao Road from the main compound of ASB's three early 1980s office towers. Along this street, I see stylish, upwardly mobile young people, very few bikes, and very few cars. It's could easily be an Italian suburb, with a bit of light industry thrown in.

It's hard for me to believe I'm finally about to visit a Chinese factory. I've wanted to do this for decades, and in my head I'm expecting a massive prison-like structure with a bogus Kentucky Fried Chicken outlet attached, all surrounded by fields of bok choy protected with barbed-wire fencing. Inside the factory? Lava. Whips. Charcoal. Foodlessness. Manacles. Framed oversized photos of Pat Nixon. What do I find instead? A long, low, pale yellow warehouse building, where I meet the charming Emanuele Cavallaro, fifty-two, Vice President of Global Manufacturing, who hands me a pair of anti-static shoe guards to ward against sparks that might damage fragile electronic wares.

Cavallaro's office overlooks a very pleasant open-plan *Mad Men*-esque office space with a pistachio-green color scheme. As he and I prepare to enter the factory proper, we discuss China's manufacturing capacity. Mr. Cavallaro tells me his theory that China is now where Germany was in 1955. "Technologically, China's leaped ahead twenty years in only five." And then we hit the moment of truth: he opens the factory doors and ... and it's among the most spotless places I've ever been. Dust-proof, zero humidity, and a pleasant 66 degrees Fahrenheit 365 days a year. It's the cleanest place I've been in the thirty-three years since friends and I got baked and

attended a Pink Floyd laser show at the local plane-
tarium where they always made such a big deal about
venue's air quality before beginning with *The Dark
Side of the Moon*. The factory is vast. Small groups
of staff in pale-blue jumpsuits attend to the shiny
objects that pop out of one quiet robotic machine to
be placed into another robotic machine. For some
reason, I'm expecting Jason Bourne to leap from the
top of one machine onto the next, in charged flight
from CIA elites gone rogue. The entire place reeks of
Japanese-level quality control, and wordlessly show-
cases China's determination to stop being the Old
China and quickly become the New China.

Mr. Cavallaro shows me the 7950 Extensible
Routing System (XRS), switching modules being
created through what is called surface mounting
technology. They'll offer five times the density of
existing alternatives while consuming only one-third
the electricity. With support for up to eighty 100GE
ports in a single track, the 7950 XRS shatters current
density norms and paves the way for scaling the ser-
vice-provider cloud infrastructure. Regardless, these
7950 XRS units progress in front of my eyes from
tiny individual components to an ever more complex
solid-state finished product packed in boxes, ready
for shipping overseas. Everywhere I look, plasma TVs
spray out statistics and oscilloscopic data confirming
that everything is okay. If only the real world could
be so easily monitored.

The factory is also q-u-i-e-t. Mr. Cavallaro
and I can easily speak. I mention my worries about
sustainability and wonder if there's anything China
can do to bubble-proof itself.

Cavallaro says, "Growth at 6 or 7 percent is
creating a lot of social issues, and it obviously cannot
be maintained indefinitely. The government's now
trying to create internal consumption within China
so as to diversify and stabilize the economy against
foreign dependency." (The thing about China is that
everyone there starts to sound sloganeerish after a
while. The language of industrial pep-speak is so

relentless that it infects even the most banal conversations. *Can I get you a drink? No, I'm already enbevulated, but thank you for your most generous and gracious kindness.*)

I can't help but wonder why this router factory is located in Shanghai and not in North America. Let me rephrase that: I understand very *well* why it's located in Shanghai, but not why there isn't *also* one located in Michigan, where 10 million primates needing 2,500 calories a day are sitting on top of a cold rock in the middle of the North American continent, and they've got nothing to do all day except go online and watch porn, TED videos, and bit-torrented movies, and then maybe go turn a trick or score some Oxy out by the interstate, behind the closed Denny's that's covered in weathered plywood. Is North America to become what China is now ceasing to be, a place where you might as well work for thirty cents an hour making baubles because there's absolutely nothing else to do except shop from your jail cell?

Earlier, Paul Ross and I were discussing the French being French and the Norwegians being Norwegians. What about Michiganders being Michiganders? When I look at Detroit or Flint or Lansing, I am forced to ponder the meaning of being alive at all: we wake up, we do something, we go to sleep, and we repeat it about 22,000 more times, and then we die. In Michigan, a North American feels a sense of losing one's coherent view of the world. In Shanghai, one senses calm hands holding the reins, even if the cart is going 10,000 miles per hour. China skipped much of what the twentieth century held for the rest of the planet, and this has left it with nothing to weigh it down as it careens futureward. One wonders when China will start opening factories in the United States. It feels inevitable. The United States is ruled by politicians. China is ruled by economists.

5

I'm in a funk as Cavallaro and I leave the factory floor. I say good-bye and cross Ningqiao Road back to ASB's corporate campus, where I'm to meet with Peter Xu, Head of Pacific Rim Hardware Sales. He exudes the energy, optimism, and drive of the nation's under-forties. His Western first name alone is a telltale sign of China's quickly morphing society. I ask Peter what changes he's noticed during his decade or so within China's tech and business worlds. He pauses and thoughtfully replies, "Meetings. So many *meetings*."

Ahhh ... meetings. Those spiritual cattle slaughter facilities where so many of our cherished dreams go to die hideous protracted deaths.

"China is now having to service the things that it makes, and with this service sector there's a huge new upwardly mobile meritocracy—and this is important: China needs to start spending money within China if our economy is to stabilize and diversify. We have to start buying the things we make." This seems to be one of the day's themes.

Xu's office is filled with trophies and boxes of swag ("Here, have a handful of free pens"), and the space has the vibe of belonging to someone with ambition. "I really am surprised at how much follow-up work there is to the sale of something. China doesn't have much history with that sort of thing."

Xu travels a lot on business, often within China, and what irks him most about his job isn't his work but, oddly (or maybe not) the hotels he has to stay in while traveling: the countless 200-renminbi-a-night (about $30) hotels catering to China's mobile working class, 200 renminbi being the amount China has decided is to be spent per night on business hotels. Xu is a smart guy—he's been abroad, and he goes to hotels.com like anyone else—and he knows what's possible. Even a Motel 6 with a broken water heater and a freeway off-ramp to lullaby him to sleep would be better than most 200-renminbi-a-night hotels. "The company has been in survival mode for so long, and I sometimes wonder if there will ever be a 'normal' again."

There's a framed photo of Xu's seven-year-old son on his shelf (the terry-cloth handcuffs strike again). I ask Xu what's the main difference between himself at the age of seven and his son at that age. "Oh, that's easy," Xu says, smiling, "He believes the Internet is the real world."

I now go to meet another Mr. Xu—Wuang Xu, fifty-three, and no relation to Peter. Wuang Xu is Director of Research and New Technologies. He learned computing on a Romanian computer in 1982. In my head, I try to imagine what a 1982 Romanian computer could possibly have looked like, but all that comes to mind is Battersea Power Station as it appears on the cover of Pink Floyd's 1977 album, *Animals.*

Xu has seen massive amounts of change in his lifetime. "Almost always I'm amazed by how things have changed. Phone calls were extreme luxuries back in 1980—but even then the future was clear to us: IP, mobile, digital, and broadband."

When China began to rejoin the world in the early 1980s, it formed a strategic alliance with Belgium's ITT. When Alcatel bought ITT in 2002, they got Alcatel Shanghai Bell in the process, a deal that allowed them entry into China on a massive scale, and a deal that may one day make the Louisiana Purchase pale in comparison.

I ask Xu if Chinese people wonder about the political changes that could be triggered by giving every man, woman, and child in China mobile Internet access. His answer is, "No."

This is actually the single weirdest thing I'm noticing about the New China and its astonishing drive to a near future where Wi-Fi and wireless merge, a bold and bright place where even a rice farmer can sit in a remote mountain cave and watch Anne Hathaway in HD in *The Devil Wears Prada*, and pause here and there to make sure he doesn't miss any Anna Wintour references: a complete lack of McLuhanesque inquiry into whether this is actually such a hot idea, and what the societal fallout might be. A return to warlord feudality? A perpetual shopping mall? Shotgun-wielding hyperlibertarianism? North Korean randomness? This sort of introspection is nonexistent, or perhaps it has already been discussed high up the food chain and it was decided best not to share the results of the conversation with the public. All China knows now is: speed = good. By 2015, all Chinese citizens will be mobile-equipped. That same year, the amount of data transmitted on cell phones will equal the amount of data transmitted online. It is relentless. It is unstoppable. There is nothing like this in the history of the world.

My final meeting is with Mr. Yangqio Chen and his assistant Julia. Mr. Chen is VP of the local Communist Party, but is also President of ASB, roles that seem contradictory at first. But, as mentioned a few pages back, the West is run by politicians, while China is run by economists, which is why phrases such as "market communism" are no longer oxymorons. Both Mr. Chen and Julia speak English perfectly. Mr. Chen wears a beautifully made blue suit, while Julia is in a stylish dress and jacket from the school of Chanel. Although seemingly prepared for a debauched afternoon of capitalism in a Singapore or London boardroom, the two are both ideologues and distinctly proud of the strides China has made. Chen says, "China didn't open up to the world until after the political reforms of 1949. It took a great deal of time for well over a billion people to stabilize, but we did finally reach the point where men and women became equal, where regional politics were homogenized, and where everyone had something to eat and something to do. So instead of being a mess, we were unified. If you want to see how unified we are now, look at China, then look at India."

I ask about the methods used to get China from 1949 to 2012. Chen says, "We looked and saw that we had to grow three things: transportation, energy, and telecommunications. The central government could either do it alone or they could open up—and so they decided to open up. That's how ASB was born; through our initial partnering with ITT."

Julia adds, "Cell phones accelerated the progress on our fixed-line course. A phone in your house took a year's salary in 1980. Soon, every person in China will have a mobile phone and access to broadband."

And Chen: "We in China were able to jump over many generations of technology. By the 1990s our landlines had caught up to those of the rest of the world. And then we started going mobile in the 1990s, as part of a Five-Year Plan. The next stage is for everything to merge: no difference between local and long-distance, and 4G-PDX optical broadband to every home in the country. We call this project 'Broadband China.'"

I feel like I've been ripped out of one time stream and implanted into another.

Chen continues, "Broadband is a new form of infrastructure. Penetration creates much more social potential in all areas of society, and we believe the changes are more positive than negative."

Chen and Julia are radiant, and Chen's last comment does, in part, answer my question as to whether the Chinese have discussed the political and social implications of giving high-speed communication technologies to the masses. I don't know what their conclusions were, but their implementation can only transform our entire species, either directly or indirectly.

I get to thinking about optical fiber in general. It's very expensive and politically difficult to put into place. ("Get your bobcat diggers off my land!") In spite of this, some financial companies are building their own optical fiber networks. The most legendary cable is one that stretches in an almost straight line from New York City to Chicago. There's another cable between the two cities, but it isn't straight. It makes turns and zigzags and changed directions enough times that light passing through it arrived five millionths of a second more slowly than light passing through a straight cable (a time period called "latency"). In a world of almost entirely computerized stock transactions, this tiny latency can give a billion-dollar trading advantage over the owners of a crooked cable. I don't want this to come out sounding breathless and full of wonder. It's hard to have much respect for a system where merit or value is based on this sort of absurdity. Surely, somewhere, a revolution must be in the works to topple this sad financial system.

I'm back in the room listening to Chen and to Julia. I'm trying to focus on mental pictures of the future, but I'm no longer sure what I'm seeing or feeling. It isn't dread. It isn't fear. The future actually feels like that awkward moment between when a practical joke has been played on you and the moment you realize that it's a practical joke. I try to think about the future with clarity, separating my predictions from my desires. I *want* the future to be a lot like the present, because on a per capita basis, the present is still the best place the human species has ever had. My prediction is that things will get worse. Maybe not bad, but not likely much better—a great plateauing. I very much worry that with all these photons being bandied about the planet, money is going to stop working one day. Money will wake up, take a look at the world, and say, "You know what? This is crazy. I'm not going to work today." I don't mean deflation or hyperinflation, simply money no longer functioning. If building a straight glass filament from Chicago to New York—as opposed to a zig-zagged filament— gives you a five-millionths-of-a-second advantage to make billions of dollars, then I don't see the idea of the End of Money as too silly at all.

Nor do I see the end of party-style politics as being absurd. The Internet ultimately makes you more of an individual than it does a member of a pack. Most people don't mind being yanked around and manipulated a bit by polarized news stations, and the stupidity of the ideas some people will believe is sometimes shocking, but all in all, that yanking dumbness is canceled out slightly by individuality. What is absolutely assured in the future is a global monoclass, equal in its access to information, and almost certainly all living in situations that are a huge letdown from the quality of life enjoyed by the twentieth century's middle classes.

I think of all the people I know who are addicted to the Internet—most everybody, really—and how the thought of being without it is impossible. And I think about my maxim that "you can either have information or you can have a life, but you can't have both," and I wonder if the goal of the future is to prove that maxim false. If information gets smarter, and when machines really do begin talking to other machines, maybe we will engineer an Internet where people no longer feel swamped or overwhelmed or constantly anxious about being culled from the pack.

I wonder about religion. The Internet indeed crystallizes and enhances tribes and communities, but their constituent components are individuated human beings who, by themselves, can go to daily mail.co.uk or nytimes.com or to a cat-breeding website or wherever else they want. You can see what's being withheld from you. You can't play dumb anymore, and that does make it harder for you to be manipulated. As for whether the Internet occupies the physical neurological slot in your head where religion and politics used to be stored, I think that metaphorically, at least, it does, if not with neurons and ganglions. (Though I suspect there are a lot of wires in the head being rerouted as surely as there are fiber cables laid from Sydney across the Pacific and onto the Oregon coast, then upriver into Google's massive server farm on the Columbia River.) Organizations are going to have to work much harder and more craftily to pluck you away from the world.

Question: Is the Internet-triggered neural rejigging of our species's brains a superficial reflection of reality? Or is it a profound change? Most people who had kids before 1995 would say it's superficial. Those with children born after 1995 would violently disagree with them.

6

After leaving Mr. Chen's office, I almost have time sickness, as though I really have wormholed into a future time slot. A few hours later, I'm at dinner directly above the Bund, a trillion dollars worth of real estate and LED lighting that blows Tokyo into the weeds. The steaks are from Argentina and cost $100 apiece. There are thirty different kinds of single-malt Scotch. The air outside the window is boiling and muggy and has that slightly damaged feeling, like a big car with a large dent in it that makes you wince and say, "Ow."

So, then, what are we learning about ourselves from all of this that we didn't know before? Off the cuff, a few things: We are more curious than we gave ourselves credit for. We like being connected to others far more than I might have guessed in 1992. We are good at finding information we need when we really need it. We have better senses of humor than I might ever have guessed. We're perhaps even kinder than we gave ourselves credit for. And we all want to be heard.

As I eat my steak, I look out the restaurant windows toward the power plants that are burning the coal from British Columbia that fuels the air conditioners and elevators and routers and switching devices and laptops and mainframes and hard drives and cell rechargers, but I know I won't see those plants, neither at night nor during the day, when the sky goes chalky white from particulates. Take away even a fraction of the speed we currently use to keep our system going, and it all falls to pieces. Or fail to maintain the infrastructure's capacity and our societies fall to pieces. So much of what defines us and our cultures is made possible by unglamorous glass threads and electric switches purposefully located in the most boring, low-profile places possible. Most people haven't heard of Alcatel-Lucent, and I wonder if it's a low profile the firm willfully fosters. It is largely a company of good-natured scientists who are quite competitive among themselves, and who like simplifying complex problems and then solving them and then moving on to the next problem. They are creating a platform technology; whatever you do with it is *your* business, and many of the scientists I spoke with were surprised to even be asked the question.

I get to thinking about energy consumption and energy usage. Twenty years ago the Internet used zero percent of the world's energy. This year it used 4 percent. This doesn't sound like much, but one must remember that a relatively short time ago it was *zero*. All these particles of incinerated British Columbia filling the sky, soaking up heat, melting the ice caps, relieving trillions of tons of weight from the two poles, allowing the planet's tectonic plates to shake themselves like a dog shaking off water, triggering a new age, the Age of Earthquakes, a world of perpetual Fukushimas and tsunamis.

In five years, the numbers in this essay will look absurdly small, and much of what is discussed will be obsolete. If you look at magazine articles from 1994, the word "Internet" is still in italics. Embarrassing phrases like "information superhighway" are discussed with the same sort of straight faces we currently use when describing the Higgs boson. I look back at myself two decades ago, and I think of how different I was in the ways I looked at the world and communicated with others. The essential "me" is still here ... it just relates to the universe so much more differently. So what will we do when a doodad the size of a peanut contains every book ever written and essentially costs nothing to make? What will happen when everything becomes anything becomes everywhere becomes all things? We're almost there.

I guess humanity is at a magic halfway point right now. I remember Peter Xu's comment that his seven-year-old son believes the Internet is the real world. Right now, half of humanity—the younger half—believes the Internet is reality. And the other half? They simply haven't yet reached the point where they, too, accept that the Internet is the real world. But they will.

George Washington's Extreme Makeover

On vacation a few years back I chose to read a very long and very worthy biography of George Washington. It had been a crazy year, and, to be honest, I chose the book because I was staying at someone's house and it was the one book I could find in their shelves that I could be sure contained no technology: no e-mail, no phones, no planes, no smoking hot Wi-Fi, no anything. On this level, the book delivered in a big way, and for a good two weeks I had a pleasant brain holiday, one that I now look back on and see almost as a form of ecotourism—visiting a place where there was a guarantee of relief from one's own daily ecosystem.

I learned that George Washington was, by any standards, a worthy fellow, and possibly one of the few competent human beings in an era when life was short and most people were largely drunk on badly made homemade cider and acidic political bromides—an era when healthy people caught a cold one afternoon and were dead by the next morning. (One interesting fact garnered from the book is that in his later years, Benjamin Franklin had severe gout and was carried around Philadelphia in a litter propelled by four black men, much in the way modern meritocrats are driven around in Bentleys.) Most importantly I learned that were it not for Washington, there would most definitely never have been a United States, so the man's historical worthiness is undebatable and the guy is just basically one of those people who changed the world. So, good for him.

Washington also had dreadfully bad teeth and spent much of his time, whenever visiting new cities, inquiring about local dentists and new procedures that might allow him to not live in near perpetual dental pain and discomfort. One reason there is no image of Washington smiling is that the man never smiled; he didn't want his teeth, or lack thereof, to show. And although he was graced by good health— he died in 1791 at the age of seventy-four, a true accomplishment for the era—he was not blessed with sound bodily comfort; as with anybody of his era, he endured his share of slow-healing wounds, fungal infections, gastrointestinal distress, and many things that can these days be nipped in the bud by a quick trip to a drug store.

But it was in reading about Washington's chronic bodily discomfort that I began to have a fantasy, one in which George, at the age of forty-five, and utterly sick of being sick, covered in lice and exhausted from having to rescue his inept countrymen from peril after peril, is teleported from atop his horse somewhere in the slave-friendly Virginia countryside, and into a Level 3 cleanroom 500 feet beneath that exact same spot 250 years later, circa

2013. Once there, he is given a big hit of Valium and told by a gentle off-screen woman's voice that he has been whisked away by angels to heal his body and better prepare him fully for the task of creating and leading a new nation. At this point, a crew of doctors, dentists, and exodontists wearing hazmat suits descend on Washington and begin futzing about with his body, identifying rashes, cysts, abscesses, growths, aches, pains, and every other form of malady, and then goes about fixing everything. Washington—I'm going to start calling him George here—is totally okay with this invasion because, hey, these are angels! No, they're not necessarily winged, but a sterile pure-white twenty-first-century environment could definitely read as a form of heaven to someone from 250 years before.

A big part of this makeover and healing fantasy would be to ensure that George doesn't catch any twenty-first-century bugs—hence the hazmat outfits. Over the course of about two weeks, George would undergo a rigid antibiotic regimen to remove any blood cooties he may have been harboring. This would then allow for the safe implantation of thirty-two dazzling new teeth using steel-post-implantation. And along the way George's skin would be moisturized, defungicized, deloused, and gently kissed a nice honey-bronze color by tanning rays—but, as Washington is a redhead (a not commonly known fact), George's makeover team has to go easy on the UV rays. George would need to look like he'd spent a week poolside in Tampa; a cocoa brown tan would look odd in 1755, and instead of making George look like a member of the ruling elites, it would make him resemble a farm laborer.

Pretty much the only thing that might complicate this makeover scenario would be if George were to fall in love with one of his hazmat angels—a twist that would please the heart of any Hollywood producer, but one that would utterly invalidate the mission of George's bodily makeover. One simply couldn't have George pining to return to heaven to reunite with, say, the sinewy and lithe Doctor Jennifer Crandall, a parasitologist with a chip on her shoulder and a quivering lower lip (to be played by Charlize Theron).

As an added bonus, Theron could undergo a radical makeunder (Oscar bait!) in order to travel back in time to reunite with George, but in going backward, she brings all sorts of contemporary flus and colds with her that decimate the US population, effectively destroying history. Only a bit of time travel trickery allows history to be saved, but fortunately, *Alien*-like, when Theron returns to the present, she's pregnant with George's child. As an added twist, the Bush family could buy the child on the black market and the Bush dynasty would once again be in the ascendant. To be honest, this is the sort of movie that can be designed by a set of novelty screenwriting fridge magnets, but it does demonstrate, even poetically, the power of DNA to transcend time.

Moving forward: George's rogue ear and nose hairs would be trimmed. His dandruff would be Selsun'ed into oblivion and George's signature Warhol-in-drag hairstyle would be fluffed and primped into Sassoon-like perfection. He'd become borderline hot, and just before leaving the Level 3 containment area, George would be given Lasik treatment to correct his vision, as well as small hits of Botox to loan him a slightly more youthful appearance. The garments he was wearing when he was absconded would have been dry-cleaned and stored for forty-eight hours at minus 144 degrees Celsius and then thawed, dried, and restitched together. Basically, when George is returned back onto his horse, back into slave-friendly Virginia, he would be a new man. This new man would be one super healthy stud and be totally ready to kick some British ass.

Fantasy over.

Or is it?

Reading about George's lifelong bodily discomfort made me wonder about history in general, and how even life's simplest bodily discomforts can have extreme historical implications—but ultimately, reading George's biography got me to wondering about what happened to George's physical body. Maybe a scan of George's DNA could tell us more than that he was a right-handed heterosexual redhead. Maybe a DNA scan could give us a genetic reading as to George's predilection for depression, for his predilection for bipolarity, or who knows what—Tay-Sachs disease? Hoarding? Fear of spiders? That's the magic of DNA ... once decoded it gives and it gives and it gives, and our future only promises ever more precise ways of reading our genetic sequences.

Back in 1789, modern cremation didn't exist so George must have been embalmed. Was he interred in a tasteful marble crypt? Did anyone think to preserve a few of his tissue samples? Probably not. Of course not.

Why would they?

And here's what I then got to thinking: growing up one is always made aware of the dodo bird specimen kept in the Victoria and Albert Museum in London. As DNA technology progresses, every week, I'm sure, the museum must be inundated with requests for just the smallest, teensiest sample of dodo DNA. At this point there can't possibly be much remaining of this sad lonely dodo and yet the requests will probably be coming in weekly for the next thousand years.

And I think all of us have seen documentaries of woolly-mammoth carcasses being disinterred whole and frozen for 10,000 years from deep within the Siberian muskeg, zipped off to Helsinki, Stockholm, or Saint Petersburg to have whatever frozen DNA remaining stored in a manner that can keep it entirely intact for the ultimate purpose of cloning.

But, back to George: can we clone him? Probably not. A woolly mammoth has a much better chance of being cloned owing to nothing more than its long-term refrigeration versus the DNA-killing high temperatures of a marble crypt in Virginia.

So what is it, then, that we've lost in the losing of George Washington's DNA? Or, is it a loss? Perhaps it's a blessing. Maybe not knowing too much about a person's body is a good thing. Maybe allowing the subject of any biography to be a product of nurture and fate is enough to create a full life.

But I really doubt it.

Dead or Canadian?

In the late 1980s, a young MTV produced a game show called *Remote Control*. It didn't last very long, but it was fun while it lasted. It was a sort of pop culture *Jeopardy!*. Instead of asking the name of the world's third largest freshwater body of water (Lake Baykal), *Remote Control* asked contestants who the least popular of the four Monkees (Peter Tork) was. If you were in the right mood at the right time of day, *Remote Control* was perfect viewing, and one of its recurring question categories was: "Dead or Canadian?"—which is to say, they'd put up a photo of, say, Glenn Ford, Eugene Levy, or Doug McLure, and contestants had to determine if they were, well, dead or Canadian (dead, Canadian, dead). Contestants almost always got the answer wrong, and as a category, American contestants must surely have dreaded being stuck with this one.

Fifteen years after *Remote Control* was canceled, my phone rang; it was 2005. I still had a landline and I still answered it. On the other end was John Saul, a Canadian author, historian, and public intellectual who was assembling a collection of biographies of "dead Canadians written by living Canadians." He wanted me to write about Marshall McLuhan and in my head I felt as if I'd landed the MTV jackpot: dead *and* Canadian.

Like most people, I knew nothing of Marshall McLuhan—except that he had coined two aphorisms: (1) "the media is the message," and (2) the notion that the world is a "global village." McLuhan died in December of 1980, during my first year of art school, and his star at that point was at its all time low; his name was never mentioned in any classes on theory or semiotics. I told all of this to Saul and asked why he wanted *me* to write about McLuhan and not somebody else. His reply was (after the briefest of pauses) that I would probably enjoy McLuhan's ideas but also that I was an embodiment of McLuhan's notions about the future. I was unsure if this was a put-down or a put-up, and I declined to do the book, but Saul was persistent and two years later I thought, okay, this could be interesting, and so I agreed to write it.

So the first thing to do was to actually read McLuhan's books to see what the man was all about. I didn't want to read anything biographical about him until I'd established some form of intellectual connection, and I thought this would be easy, but it wasn't. The first thing I learned about McLuhan is that almost nobody has read his books because, in certain structural ways, they are almost unreadable. They are opaque and repetitive; they digress endlessly, revel in ontological cul-de-sacs, and draw relentlessly on a vast and staggering number of classical sources that are themselves almost challengingly tangential. The man can go on for ages on a technicality—Elizabethan pamphleteers, say—and yet dismiss something like all of twentieth-century art in one sentence.

McLuhan's two masterpieces were 1961's *Gutenberg Galaxy*, and 1964's *Understanding Media*. *Gutenberg Galaxy* is a neutron-star chunk of a book that a typical reader could enter into for perhaps two pages at a time before slamming it down in anger—or perhaps cradle it to his or her chest in a swoon of new perceptions. My copy of the book is laced in the margins with comments like: *what an asshole*, and *this is great*. It is probably the most combative read I've ever had, and ever will.

Both *Gutenberg Galaxy* and *Understanding Media* are vast, cryptic, extemporaneous, and dizzying, yet glacial. Intellectually, McLuhan's books offer a sumptuous Louis XIV banquet of ideas in which one occasionally finds a folding card table offering stale oatmeal cookies and room temperature lemonade. Or a fifteen-cent-off coupon for Jell-O. Or peacock McNuggets.

Basically, McLuhan predicted and described the Internet in 1961, but because he couldn't describe the Internet's websites and technical specifics like Google, eBay, or PayPal, he came across to people as though he were slightly nuts. In 2013 we've all become accustomed to master theory books like *Guns, Germs, and Steel*, *The Age of Extremes*, and *Blink*. Such books are lucid and written in an almost conversational tone, allowing for easy access to the ideas presented. No such luck with McLuhan, and before finishing *Understanding Media* I was able to see why he was invariably reduced to his two main clichés: anything else would take forever to explain.

After having read McLuhan's books, I knew then that the heavy lifting had to begin, and that I'd have to read two preexisting McLuhan biographies, both of which, unfortunately for their authors, were written pre-Internet. And then I'd have to make a timeline of McLuhan's life and write, well, a *biography*.

Being a first-time biographer, my initial strategy in reading about McLuhan's life was to enter McLuhan's mind and body and find something, anything, that the two of us had in common, and build from there. This might have been very difficult were I to be writing about Hermann Göring, Susan B. Anthony, or Aung San Suu Kyi, but with Marshall McLuhan I hit the jackpot. First, his family's ancestral and immigration experience was a direct copy in time and space of that of my own family: Bible-thumping Scotch-Irish traversing the nineteenth- and twentieth-century Canadian Maritimes and prairies. (McLuhan even lived down the street from my mother in Winnipeg; they attended the same high school. I suppose this overlap is a benefit of me being a living Canadian writing about a dead Canadian.) Second, McLuhan's medical eccentricities and tics in some ways mirrored many of my own, sometimes to a level that was spooky—particularly when one approaches the lower end of the autistic spectrum, that magic line where personality becomes pathology.

This second overlap very much helped me to bond with someone who was, by any description, very hard to bond with. Remember, McLuhan's ship came in when he was fifty years old. He was a crusty, highly Catholic fuddy-duddy teacher of Middle English at the University of Toronto. He had many of the uncomfortable prejudices of his era (just think of your parents ranting on at the Thanksgiving table). He would discuss his ideas almost anywhere at any time, but he never *ever* discussed his beliefs or his fears or his sense of himself. Not that one needs do that, but it certainly makes it harder to open the gate. I got the impression that if I met McLuhan at a dinner party he'd be fascinating for the first ten minutes and then highly annoying for the next 180, and the only way to get through those minutes would be to perform a sort of psychiatric armchair analysis along the lines of, "What the heck is going on inside this guy? Why is he always punning?" McLuhan loved puns, but punning is actually shown to be a wiring glitch in regions of the brain where ideas are turned into words that are then turned into sounds that are then spoken by the mouth. (Oddly, McLuhan's only million-seller was a highly art-directed musing on his ideas by graphic designer Quentin Fiore; McLuhan provided only the title: *The Medium is the Massage*—a pun.)

McLuhan had many wiring glitches. Everyone does. There is no "normal," but there are standard deviances. This is undeniable. With almost scientific clarity we can say that McLuhan had a low- to medium-grade case of Asperger's syndrome. In social situations he was bombastic. His interaction skills were poor; his classes were filled with tripping hippies whom he loathed, and who looked at McLuhan in much the same spirit as current students might view a payload of Mentos being dropped into a bottle of Diet Coke. The thing is, whether in a classroom or at a dinner table, McLuhan was pretty much a one-way leaf blower of ideas and theories. He also suffered from hyperacuity (extreme sensitivity to noise). He was an astonishing mimic—a skill he inherited from his mother, and a skill related to hypervascularization of certain portions of the brain. This is where this story becomes like science fiction: McLuhan had a third artery in his head that ran through his brain's left lobe, a vascularization feature of mammals only ever seen in cats. It was discovered when he had a lemon-sized brain tumor removed in 1968. McLuhan also had pronounced memory skills—a condition that occurs when factual information is stored in the portion of the brain otherwise used for wayfinding and directionality. For people who remember pi to ten thousand digits, they're not telling you a numerical sequence; in their minds they're simply giving you driving instructions. And finally, McLuhan possessed a sense of what some psychiatric community members call "Christmas Morning Syndrome"—the perpetual enviable sense that one is in the midst of a holy or numinous situation, something most people experience a few times in their lives; McLuhan lived it 24/7. He was a daily attender of mass and put up with the late twentieth century only because upon death, he would be able to escape it.

But let's focus on autism, which, in the early twenty-first century, is certainly a jumping-off point for endless discussions on the medicalization of the personality, which I have absolutely no problem with, but (I learned) many people do. I looked at my own family's experiences across the 150 or so years for which we have stories, and, just like in your family, mine has its own ghosts and legends and people who magically vanish. Certain people are either never discussed, or if they are, a life and a legacy are washed away with phrase like "Him? He took to his bed and never left," or, "She had the vapors, and was never the same again," or, "He was ... *troubled*. We never saw him much. Why would you want to talk about him, anyway?"

But to view recent ancestors through the lens of SSRI drugs, painkillers, or Cipro is to force one to have true compassion. The vapors is depression. Taking to one's bed is atrial fibrillation. The village idiot was bipolar. Your reclusive uncle was hermetic, which probably meant he was socially phobic and merely somewhere on the low end of the autism spectrum. Did I say "merely"? That's where this gets contentious. To describe someone by a condition is to somehow diminish their humanity, when, in fact, I believe, it allows us to know why they were the way they were and to allow us to feel greater compassion for them. Your great grandmother by the lake wasn't possessed by the devil; she had an anxiety disorder. A cure was just a molecule away. Poor thing.

So when it came to Marshall and writing about the man, I felt the need to look at autism head on, that to not do so would be irresponsible, and I even went so far as to include (with permission) a reader-participation autism "test" created by British autism researcher Simon Baron-Cohen. I also investigated punning, alliteration, rhyming, and other brain anomalies that, in concert, define a person's speech and much of what we call personality. In so doing I ended up reframing many of the ways I look at myself and the people around me. Do I see myself or others as walking "conditions"? Well, sort of. Do I see someone who whistles while they work as having a medical condition? Yes. But it doesn't make that person any less endearing—I merely know why it's happening. (A human tic can almost always be ascribed to a brain wiring glitch, or in the amount of blood certain regions of the brain receive.)

Would I do the biography differently were I to do it again? Absolutely. Live and learn.

Would I be as medically forensic were I to do the book again? Absolutely. Even more so, actually. I think that any biographer from here on would be doing a disservice to their subject, their reader, and themselves to not attempt some form of forensic reconstruction of their subject's physical and psychological pathologies. This is not to say there isn't magic and poetry that arises from all of these glitches and malfunctions. I do see McLuhan as a poet, and it's to our species's credit that even though most people had no idea what McLuhan was on about, they realized that it was *something* valuable and something worth keeping.

Again, in many ways McLuhan was the antithesis of what society thought he was, a future-loving technology-crazed booster of high-speed change. Wrong. He despised the twentieth century and saw technology as the undoing of the human species and the planet. His utopia would be to live in a kingdom without borders, in a world before the printing press—a world of yarns and stories and troubadours—a world in which one wouldn't even consider the voices in their heads as their own, but rather the voices of dead relatives or the king stopping by for a chat and then moving on. This sort of universe is an "aural" universe where the spoken word trumps all. Whether it was wishful thinking or not, McLuhan saw the successor technology to the television as being the technology (the Internet) that would take us back to the world of the ear. It can sound so simple but he made it sound so impenetrable.

He was a man far ahead of his time and a man far behind his time—he was never actually *in* his time.

McLuhan's son Eric, now seventy-three, was kind enough to give me an inner cheek swab of his buccal cells which I then sent to a genetic research company to find out more about McLuhan genetics from this direction. I was told (three weeks later) that the subject came from Ireland/Scotland/England. *Quelle surprise*, BUT, for an extra $169.99 I could pay to have a matrilineal DNA amplification package that could net me far more targeted results—which is when I learned that much of the DNA industry is as big a scam as theater popcorn or weekend mattress-blowout sales. Eric's DNA is on file and some day, when getting your genetic map printed is as common as laser printing a sign advertising lost kittens, we can revisit Eric McLuhan's DNA and learn something of his father.

Does any of McLuhan's DNA survive? Possibly. McLuhan was buried in January of 1981 in Holy Cross Cemetery in northern Toronto. In 1988 I was working in Toronto as a fact-checker and up-front editor of a now long defunct business magazine. This was before fax machines broke the psychologically significant $1,000 price point. Susan McMillan from the advertising department was asking editorial to do something, anything, interesting about fax machines in order to attract fax ad sales. I actually love this kind of challenge, and in response I created the "Celebrity Fax of the Month." The first was a really lovely lipstick kiss by supermodel Linda Evangelista faxed to us from the Hotel George V in Paris on its stationery. It floated on the page like a Man Ray sketch and was really gorgeous. Unfortunately, I had eleven more celebrity faxes to do that year, and what began as fun quickly became a pain in the ass, and all of us in the junior editorial pool were scratching our heads to come up with new ideas. The series reached a simultaneous acme and nadir one month when, after the previous month's celebrity fax—a hockey puck from a recently signed NHL player faxed to us from Moscow—we printed a photocopy of a slice of Wolfgang Puck's new frozen pizza from his flagship restaurant in Beverly Hills. It's genius caption? "Last month we brought you a hockey puck. This month we bring you Wolfgang Puck!" This was when we juniors knew we were in a level of hell and we were getting desperate. To this end, I remember one incredibly cold afternoon I took the subway and then a bus way the heck out into Toronto's northern suburbs and visited McLuhan's grave with some 8.5 × 11" paper and a piece of graphite. Here's the thing: I didn't know squat about McLuhan, but I knew that he was all about technology and, well, we were all flailing to fill that wretched fax page with something, anything. So I made a rubbing of the surprisingly low-key gravestone that you can easily see on Google Images. In a then-high-tech computer font it read, "The truth shall make you free." I took the image back to the office and faxed it around the world through a chain of fax machines used by friends working in various offices abroad, until the final image returned to Toronto highly degraded yet still legible. The meaning of what I did is lost—and maybe never existed to begin with—but I look back on that day now and what really sticks in my mind is one thing: I was just six feet away from Marshall McLuhan's DNA, and maybe there's still some left.

Cloudgängers

Imagine if you could go on a date with yourself—not a sexy date—just coffee, say. And not your DNA twin version of yourself, but the one person on Earth whom some super-intelligent computer picked out to be your date. This person could possibly even be the opposite gender—but probably not, because this computer's only matchmaking criterion was to locate the person on Earth who most completely and totally resembles you in IQ, politics, religion, morality, sexual tastes, humor, childhood experience, adulthood experiences, and pretty much everything else. So the chances are your date is going to be the same gender as you. How would your date go? I think that you'd like yourself a lot. Just think of all the things you could recommend to each other—and think of all the things you could warn each other away from: movies, businesses, churches, countries, hotels, other people ... And what if you meet yourself and are disgusted? Your date could be a disaster and you end up hating yourself—but then what a quick and easy way to learn what you want to change about yourself.

But what if this supercomputer also introduced you to the next ten people like yourself. Collectively, the dozen of you would actually be just one person more or less spread across twelve bodies. And chances are you'd all probably get along quite well, too. Maybe you'd all move in together. You'd almost be like a cult house: *Ooh, it's those scary people who all think and believe everything exactly alike. Stay away.*

What if the computer selected 1,000 people just like you. Or 10,000 people. At what number would you draw the line at, "Nah—that person's just too different from me"? And here's an idea: what if, say, you were having a personal crisis and needed solid advice? Who better to go to than your calm detached doppelgängers? You could basically crowd source personal problems and ideas entirely by "yourself."

Now, let's ask what if the computer selected the one million people in your country closest to you. You could get together and form a political party and you'd have very little dissent among yourselves. Depending on your country's size, a computer could maybe even locate a 51-percent majority, the "You Party," and you would win instantly. No election needed—just a very smart computer choosing the largest possible 51 percent.

All of this isn't silly. To some extent finding your doppelgänger already exists; people just haven't figured out how to access and harvest from existing data streams. But it's an absolute certainty that within a decade you will be able to find your doppelgänger or they'll find you. The amount of data we spew out into the universe these days is multiplying logarithmically. Telecommunications experts unanimously agree that the future of data isn't you or me sending more e-mails or downloading more movies; the future of data is machines talking to other machines, and what they'll be talking about is *you*: how much you spent on gum in the past decade, when and how much you urinate and its color, which politicians you're slamming, which species of puppy you find the cutest—that's the sexy stuff. They'll also be talking to each other about your carbon footprint, how bonded you are to your hometown, which sorts of people you mistrust or what ideas bore you.

In a way it's like eHarmony.com, except instead of twenty-nine levels of intimacy, it's an infinite number of levels—and don't go knocking eHarmony.com. Those people are spooky. Pretty much every wedding I've gone to since 2001 has been courtesy of eHarmony.com. Those people know their shit, and they *get* data; data rarely lies.

This data we're talking about is being spewed out into the Cloud. Ten years ago the Cloud didn't exist and now it inarguably constitutes the largest entity our species has ever created. But the Cloud isn't a fluffy blob floating above Manhattan. The blob is made of an almost staggeringly boring and unimaginable complex assembly of wires, routers, switches, and storage drives spread around the planet, usually in big box-like structures in the dullest parts of the town you live in. There is no way to make the Cloud sexy: Brad Pitt will never star in the movie version of the Cloud. *Nobody* would star in the movie version. The movie version would be a twenty-four-hour nannycam in the ceiling of Data Containment Vault Number Seven in Google's data mothership in The Dalles, Oregon.

There is an insane amount of data being stockpiled in the Cloud and much of it is about you. But before you get paranoid, there's an insane amount of data about everybody else there as well, and in a way our data storage is like that of the former German Democratic Republic—when the Wall came down there were so many gymnasiums and storage facilities filled up with informer-provided data that it mostly ended up in bonfires of paperwork; it would have taken hundreds of years to assess all of the data the Stasi had accumulated. Now multiply all of that paperwork by 50 trillion.

However, aside from your identity being hacked, there is a more unexpected and yet also more intuitively plausible result of the future of your Cloud data. After a lifetime of you filling the Cloud with volcano loads of your personal information, all of that data will aggregate together to form a meta version of yourself—your meta-you—your *cloudgänger.*

Imagine there's a large room with two boxes in it. Your mother is sitting in a chair in front of these two boxes and she's told that one of them contains you, and one contains your cloudgänger. By talking with each of the boxes she has to figure out which is which—an elaboration on the Turing machine. Also, your cloudgänger is hooked up to a vocalizer and speaks just like you. It wouldn't be long before the real you and your cloudgänger would be arguing, trying to convince your mother you're the real one, and in the end, your mother wouldn't know the difference. That's the start of it.

Your cloudgänger will be tapeworm-like thing a trillion bits long. It will be every e-mail you've ever sent, everything you've ever purchased, your medical history, everywhere you've ever been in front of a camera, your dating patterns, your masturbation patterns, your child-rearing patterns, your voice, your inflections, the way you make typos. As an added bonus it's connected to Google and Wikipedia and the ARPANET and *Al Jazeera* and every other data trove on Earth. The only real difference between you and your cloudgänger (aside from the fact that you're made of meat and it isn't) is that it's a quadrillion times smarter than you. It knows the eighteenth root of pi. It knows the cube root of every book written in the nineteenth century. And if you attach your cloudgänger to a biometrically hyperaccurate ultra-Pixar version of your body, even your meat becomes a quibble. You've been duplicated. And then, after few decades, you get hit by a bus and die. But your cloudgänger lives on. For the people who knew you—or the other cloudgängers that knew/know you—the missing meat is no big deal, with the added bonus that *you*, as an entity, keep growing, and growing as a personality and person. You have become an app. The only thing this app does is look at the world through the lens of what was once your "personality" or your life's "story."

A lot of things could happen at this point. Your cloudgänger could be erased or deleted. Your cloudgänger could go to war with another cloudgänger and kill it, only to feast on its stored data. Your cloudgänger could merge with other cloudgängers. Your cloudgänger could make copies of itself, billions if it so wished. In my mind I'm seeing a planet covered by Tesla waves of electricity, every person born since 2010 coexisting at once, arguing and solving crossword puzzles and yacking away endlessly. Or maybe they're not. The missing ingredient here is sentience: that magic moment when the spark of life—self-awareness—leaves the human body and is free to roam the planet with its own agenda, and the most logical place for it to adapt and make expressions of itself is to hijack cloudgängers—*your* cloudgänger, perhaps.

We're conditioned to view sentience as a more or less friendly HAL 9000-like entity with the voice of a country doctor. Or the voice of a wise mother cooing at a newborn. But I find that hard to imagine. Like anything alive, sentience must first exist as an embryo—which is what today's electronic world really is, a womb—and then a newly evolved sentience would need to have a birth, an infancy, an adolescence, and a mature life. I find it very hard to believe that something newly born would, right out of the gate, see its first and overriding goal in life to bringing about the golden age of human beings. It'll instead do the cyber equivalent of shitting its diapers and scream for attention. The birth of sentience is probably not going to be much fun.

Whose cloudgänger will sentience hijack first? A random cloudgänger? The cloudgänger with the highest number of Google hits (or whatever it is they have in the future)? Will newly born sentient entities try to kill other competing cloudgängers? Or mate with them? That could really be something: everyone who's ever lived since, say, 2010 merged into a collective being, an app called Humanity. And this app can make copies of itself, as many as it likes. Why not? Electrons are free and in infinite supply.

In the past, one goal in life was to leave behind a work of art or a scientific discovery from which people could glean or intuit a little bit about who you were. Or perhaps you could leave behind a story, a biography, or an autobiography that could inspire others or at least convey to future beings the sense of one's life having been a story. But what happens when the story is eclipsed by raw data? Travel patterns, shopping habits, search histories, and response times and everything else we generate? We must then reevaluate the narrative flow of our lives, and the meaning of what our stories are. Subjectively, all the current signs I see point to a new flattened perspective of personality, or of what constitutes a story—a sense of de-narration, a veering away from the romantic nineteenth- and twentieth-century notions of life's meaning. Personalities seem to be much more based on data tracks and ISP addresses, lat/longs, and everything else that will constitute your cloudgänger. You bought a pair of denim pants from an H&M at 2:17 p.m. on July 5, 2018. On December 19, 2045, you entered the words "Margaret Thatcher topless" into the search engine of the day. It doesn't take much more to establish who you probably were, and an infinite amount of computing speed could fill in biographical blanks with a scale-perfect mimic of your life. Or, a computer could print out a note-perfect redacted transcript of a life of a fictional person based solely on a pair of jeans, a goofy porn search, and a few other random-ish inputs. Billions of possible lives can be created instantly and … and then what? The planet is one great big electrical storm, pure synthetic existence, at which point it will certainly have manipulated humans into making a physical infrastructure for it that is so stable it needs no maintenance and can work perfectly for a billion years. Meat people? Extinct.

To be in a spaceship looking down on this glistening Tesla planet, this gorgeous glitterball—filled with everyone on earth since 2010 (who have been dying, being reborn and reincarnating every single moment)—one would be looking at an expression of pure existence, of one species's greatest triumph. And of course, ultimately, this sentient glitterball Earth would need to colonize the sun as a storage and data facility. In a billion years, the sun will then implode and then re-explode as a supernova. New planets would be created. Other stars would collapse and be reborn as supernovas; they would then merge with our own newly reborn sentient newborn sun and planets. Carbon atoms, guided by the knowledge embedded in their very being, begin forming complex molecules and would eventually go on to create life. Life would evolve for a further billion years, and ultimately it would climax—in the form of a seven-page *Hello!* magazine spread, "At Home with Jennifer Aniston: 'I just wanted something breezy and California'—Also Inside: The New Supersized Sharon Osbourne!"

All of which really does beg the question, are we so full of ourselves as a species that the entire universe has to be about *us?* Personally, I'd rather live in a universe run by golden Labradors or dolphins.

But will my cloudgänger think differently?

The big question here is, when do you end and someone else begin? When you first meet with your eleven other cloudgängers, will the differences between you matter much, or are you all pretty much the same person? Is individualism in this instance sort of embarrassing? Is it realistic? And what about that first group of one million cloudgängers who are closest to you … you can find safety in numbers, but only at the declining value of your uniqueness. Is uniqueness a joke? Is uniqueness replicable? If uniqueness is corny or devalued, then does private property become corny and embarrassing and deval-ued, too? And when does the good of the tribe come ahead of the good of the individual? He's into snow-mobiling. She's into 1930s Depression-era jam jars. They all love country music and those people over there want to regulate weapons and limit contracep-tion for women. Whose needs eclipse those of others? When does belief become a nightmare? When does unearned historical privilege become an inarguable right? There are way too many of us right now—the present is in no way sustainable—so how does it end? When does it end? And who will be the last human being, the last biography?

I'm sitting here writing and I feel like "me," but if a sentient computing system had my cloudgänger up and running, would "I" be beside the point? Would that mirror-me end up saying and doing and thinking the same things that I would? I don't like the notion of an app-like cloudgänger version of me, but at the same time, how great would it be to live on for a billion more years?

But, of course, that's just my ego speaking.